Teddy Bears
With a Past

Nancy Tillberg

Published by

Krause Publications
700 East State St., Iola, WI 54990-0001
Telephone 715-445-2214
www.krause.com

Please call or write for our free catalog of publications. Our toll-free number to place an order or obtain a free catalog is 800-258-0929 or please use our regular business telephone 715-445-2214 for editorial comment and further information.

Library of Congress Catalog Number 99-66144
ISBN 0-87341-856-5

Dedication

In memory of Pop.
"If you're happy and you know it make a bear!"

Acknowledgments

I would first and foremost like to thank my husband Peter for all of his support in my bear making and book writing endeavors. Without his patience and tolerance of all of the flying fluff, the late hours, and endless teddy talk, this book would never have been written. I would also like to thank my late father for all of the help and tips he provided me over the years for working with real fur, and my mother for teaching me how to sew.

A very special thank you to Stephanie Siemieniuk for contributing her talents to this book, and to Amy Pronovost for her help with the graphics. Thank you also to the publishing professionals at Krause Publications, for their always friendly voices on the phone, and their guidance and support. I also owe a very large debt of appreciation to Michelle McKenzie for getting the ball rolling for me. Although this book had been a spark in my imagination for some time, without her input, the fire would not have been lit!

And finally, I would like to acknowledge the artistic genius of my photographer Rick Novak. Rick is a fellow police officer and forensic specialist. Within these pages, however, he has given each and every teddy a pulse. I was constantly amazed how he took each bear I gave him and placed it in exactly the right setting to make it come alive. Thank you so much!

Table of Contents

ntroduction

Throughout my career as a police officer, I have seen first hand the enormous power of the teddy bear in times of crisis. It can calm a terrified child, bridge the distance between investigator and victim, and act as support in discussing difficult situations. The effect is as much the same with adults as it is with children.

Your teddy bear's appeal can be increased with your family when it is made from an old fur coat with already strong sentimental attachments. Fur has a certain elegance that gives these teddies an irresistible attraction.

Over the last five years I have taught hundreds of people from across Canada and as far away as Australia to make teddy bears. The bonding is always the same, as creator falls in love with creation. For me, teddy bear making has been a remarkable source of stress relief, and I anticipate that in my retirement years I will still be on my front porch, designing and constructing my baby bruins.

My hope is that you will enjoy making teddies as much as I do. I have written this book with the experiences of my students in mind to help you create a huggable bear on the first attempt. Whether you are using an old fur, mohair, or synthetic plush, feel free to lose yourself in the upcoming pages and enjoy the artistic process. And remember that it is never too late to have a happy childhood!

Bear Hugs,

Chapter 1

Getting Started

Getting Started

Making a teddy bear can be a very fulfilling and enjoyable process. The finished bear can be yours to enjoy for years to come, or it can make a very special gift for a friend or loved one.

In talking with students who have attended my workshops, I have found that many of them find both the assembly of the bear and the choosing of tools equally satisfying. My goal is to guide you through the process of making a beautiful, quality teddy bear that will make you proud to say, "I made it!"

Traditional bears can be made from mohair and synthetic plush. This book will give you all of the necessary information to make these teddies. In addition, I will guide you through the process of turning an old fur coat into a treasured bear-loom that you will cherish for years to come.

I would like to introduce you to Ono. In my workshops, I have found that some very frustrating errors are particularly common to bear making. Ono will help you recognize these slips before they happen, saving you much time and effort. Also keep an eye out for the numerous tips throughout the book which will help make the job even easier.

Let's begin with the tools and supplies used in bear making.

TOOLS

There are two categories, the essentials and those that are nice to have. The essentials are those tools that you must have to successfully complete your bear, while the tools that are nice to have will make the job easier (but they are not indispensable). If you plan to make many bears, you may wish to purchase some of these "extras." There is a further discussion of tools in Chapters 4 and 5.

Category One: The Essentials

- **Good sharp scissors.** This is the number one must-have!
- **Long dressmaker's pins.** These are used for pinning pattern pieces together prior to sewing.
- **Needles.** This includes long doll sculpting needles, regular sewing needles, and leather needles.
- **Needle nose pliers.** These are used for pulling stubborn stitches through the materials and for inserting glass eyes.
- **Scotch tape.** This will keep loose fur out of the way during the shaving process and while embroidering the nose.
- **Nap brush** (for example a dog grooming brush). Use it to groom your bear and to remove fur caught in the seams.

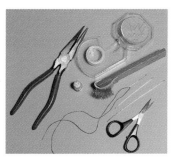

These tools are must-haves for bear making.

Category Two: Nice Tools to Have

- **Sewing machine.** All of your bear's parts can be sewn by hand, but a good machine will make short work of larger pieces.
- **Awl.** This is useful for piercing holes at joint and eye placement markings.
- **Electric shaver.** It can be used for trimming the muzzle.
- **Stuffing stick.** This beveled stick will help put stuffing into those hard-to-reach places and aid you while sculpting your bear.
- **Silver and gold markers, colored markers, chalk, or grease pens.** These are all helpful when drawing patterns onto dark-colored furs, where pen and some markers are hard to see.
- **Glycerin.** It softens old, dry furs.
- **Thimble.** Use one to protect your finger when stitching through thick leather.
- **Ratchet.** This can come in handy for tightening lock-nut joints.

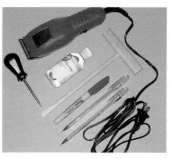

These tools are nice to have but are not essential for bear making.

Glues

Glues are not "must-haves," but you may need to use some depending on the type of bear you make. Many varieties of glue are available in craft, department, hardware, and fabric stores. If you are making a real fur bear, purchase a glue stick to help adhere the lining to the fur pattern pieces. Five-minute epoxy works well when making easy-to-use lock-nut joints. A tacky glue is useful to help secure glass and shoe-button eyes, while a small amount of white craft glue can help achieve the perfect embroidered nose. Leather glue can be used to repair small tears in real fur pelts.

There are many glues suitable for working with teddy bears.

Tip

A word to the wise about safety. Bear in mind that even parts marked "safety" can be unsafe for very young children. Glass eyes and body armatures should only be used for collectable bears that will not be played with. Never give a bear with these parts to an infant or child. Whenever you make a bear, choose only the best and most appropriate supplies with its recipient in mind.

Bear Making Materials

Synthetic Furs

Synthetic plush furs come in a wide variety of beautiful colors and textures. They are readily available at your local craft or fabric store and are relatively inexpensive. Prices for synthetic plush generally range from about $5 to $100 per yard. Imported synthetics are a little more costly, because they generally have a woven backing, which makes them very durable. Woven backings will not stretch, so your finished bear will closely resemble the pattern. Virtually all synthetics made in North America have a knit backing. Care must be taken when using these so holes for eyes and joints do not fray. Keep in mind that these knit-backed furs will stretch when stuffed.

When choosing a good-quality synthetic, look for a dense fur, through which the backing is not easily seen. Also, look for a tightly-knit or -woven backing.

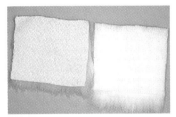

Tightly knit backing (shown at left) and woven backing (shown at right).

Hundreds of varieties of synthetic furs are available. They come in a wide range of colors and lengths; here is a small sampling.

Mohair

Mohair is the original teddy bear fabric. It is made from the wool of the angora goat that is woven onto a cloth backing. Its beauty and versatility are virtually unsurpassed in teddy bear making, and comes in an almost limitless supply of colors and tex-

A sampling of mohair; there are thousands of varieties available.

tures. It can be sparse or dense, short, long, curly, distressed, or feathered. The disadvantages of mohair are its price and availability; it ranges in price from approximately $50 to $300 per yard, and it is usually imported from England or Germany, although some domestic sources exist. It is usually found in specialty shops and teddy bear supply stores. If you do not have mohair available in your area, it can be mail ordered (see Supplies and Sources).

Reclaimed Fur Garments

Here is your chance to take an old fur coat and stuff it! Furs that work beautifully for teddy bear making include mink, muskrat, Persian lamb, seal, rabbit, and beaver. Longer furs such as fox and raccoon also make lovely bears but are more difficult to work with. Real fur is discussed in more detail in Chapter 2.

A mink coat, like this one, can be used to make a gorgeous teddy bear.

Eyes

Eyes are available in a wide variety of colors and sizes, giving each bear maker a host of looks to choose from. Plastic safety eyes are best for bears that will be given to children, while glass eyes can add sparkle to an heirloom-quality bear. Instructions for the installation of the various eyes can be found in Chapter 5.

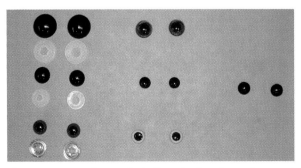

An assortment of eyes, including plastic safety, glass, and shoe button.

Plastic Safety Eyes

Plastic safety eyes are available at most craft stores and are very inexpensive. They are attached with a plastic or metal lock washer and come in many colors and sizes.

Glass Eyes

Glass eyes of various sizes can be found on a wire loop or straight wire. With the latter, you will make your own loop. Although black eyes are the most popular, many colors are available. Glass eyes lend beautiful color, depth, and sparkle to your finished bear. Because they are sewn in, they are not safe for children and will shatter if abused. Glass eyes may be purchased in teddy bear supply stores and some craft outlets.

Shoe Button Eyes

Shoe buttons, taken from early twentieth-century boots, were often used for early bears. Today, shoe button eyes, either antique or replica, can lend a vintage look to a bear. Slight imperfections in the finish are normal. Again, these eyes are sewn in, so they are not safe for children. Shoe buttons can be found in teddy bear supply stores and antique shops.

NOSES

Much like eyes, teddy bear noses come in all different shapes, sizes, and colors, and the various styles will all add individuality to your bear. You can choose from plastic safety noses, embroidered noses, or hand-made leather noses. The type of nose you decide upon will infuse a great deal of personality into your bear. Instructions for installation of the various noses and embroidery are included in Chapter 5.

Noses can be plastic, leather, or embroidered. The nose you choose will personalize your bear's character.

Plastic Safety Noses

Plastic safety noses come in a wide variety of shapes and sizes. They are fastened to the bear with an easy-to-attach backing washer and are inexpensive.

Leather Noses

Leather noses, which can be made from leather scraps, are handmade by the bear maker (a sample pattern is included in Chapter 5) and can add a real touch of character to your bear.

Embroidered Noses

Embroidered noses may take some practice to perfect; however, the result is durable, safe, and characteristic of heirloom bears. Pearl cotton works best for the embroidery because it lies flat and does not fray during sewing.

JOINTS

Teddy bear joints are the devices used to make the arms, legs, and head swivel. Again, there are several choices. The joints you choose will determine the tightness of the arms' and legs' swivel, ranging from a very loose, wobbly joint that will give your bear a well-loved appearance, to a very tight joint designed to stand up to years of loving. Joints are discussed in more detail in Chapter 6.

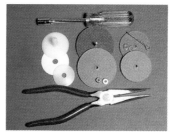

There is a wide range of joints available, including plastic safety, cotter pin, lock-nut, and pop-rivet.

Plastic Safety Joints

Plastic safety joints are a three-part system that lock into place with a simple push. They are inexpensive, easy to install, and safe for children. There is no control for the tightness of these joints, so they may loosen slightly with wear.

Cotter Pin Joints

Cotter pin joints are used with hardboard, fiberboard, or wooden disks, metal washers, and a cotter pin. The pin is inserted through the disks and washers, and its ends are

The Bear Beginnings:
A Brief History of the Teddy Bear

As early as the mid-nineteenth century, toy bears were already capturing children's hearts. These bears closely resembled real bears and were made to stand on all four paws. Early in the twentieth century, the teddy bear as we know it today was born. Few other toys have had as long a life span in their original form as the teddy. It is loved by young and old alike, and often accompanies one owner throughout his or her life. It is always willing to lend an ear, never talks back, and speaks volumes of love in every language known to man.

In November 1902, President Theodore Roosevelt refused to shoot a bear cub captured for him while on a futile hunting trip. This incident prompted political satirist Clifford Barryman to draw a cartoon depiction for the Washington Post entitled "Drawing the Line in Mississippi." The cartoon ran on November 16, 1902, and represented both the hunting expedition and a boundary dispute to which the President was committed to finding a resolution.

A short time after the cartoon was published, Russian immigrants Morris and Rose Michtom displayed a handmade teddy bear in the window of their New York novelty shop. Rose named the bear Teddy's Bear. The Butler Brothers wholesale company purchased a large number of Teddy's Bears and distributed them throughout the United States. With the financial backing of Butler Brothers, the Michtoms founded The Ideal Novelty and Toy Company.

At about the same time, a German dressmaker crippled by polio was making stuffed toy elephants from the leftover wool of women's clothing. Her nephew designed a small bear which she made into a prototype. That woman was Margaret Steiff. Originally, the bears, made of mohair, had a metal button embossed with an elephant in one of their ears. Three thousand Steiff bears were purchased, almost as an afterthought, at the Leipzig Toy Fair in March 1903 by an American toy importer. Once in America, the bears gained enormous popularity, and by 1906, with the continued influence of the Barryman cartoon bear, the era of the teddy bear had been born.

Teddy bear making firms soon began springing up all over Europe and America. The little bruins were loved by boys and girls alike, and very quickly became the international symbol of love and youthful innocence.

Although there is some debate about who originated the teddy bear, both The Ideal Novelty and Toy Company and Steiff were pioneers, but eventually, the Steiff teddy bear became the bear of choice. Early Steiff bears can command colossal sums of money at auctions, with the record being set at an auction in 1994; $174,000 was paid for the Steiff bear "Teddy Girl." The Steiff company is still producing bears and a host of other stuffed toys.

I recently had a wonderful experience after I restored a woman's childhood teddy bear. On completing the bear, I delivered it to her in the hospital where she was recuperating from an illness. She did not know I was coming, and I was unaware that this particular day was her birthday. The reunion of teddy and owner brought us both very near to tears!

I would recommend that if you own a very old teddy bear, that you have it appraised by an expert. There may be a very pleasant surprise waiting for you! However, whether the bear is young or old, give it a hug, for its value to you cannot be measured in dollars.

turned over tightly using needle nose pliers or a "cotter key." Like safety joints, they can loosen, although there is some control by the maker for tightness. Cotter pin joints are very popular and were widely used in bears from the early twentieth century. A double cotter pin joint makes for a wobbly head and appendages that can give your bear a well-loved look.

Lock-nut Joints

Lock-nut joints require the use of a screw driver and a ratchet. It can take a little practice to become comfortable with the installation. Bolts can be glued with epoxy to the disks to make the installation easier and eliminate the use of the screwdriver. These joints can be fine-tuned to the desired tightness and will not loosen with age.

Pop-rivet Joints

Pop-rivet joints are inexpensive but require a special pop-rivet tool and some practice to install. They are quite tight, and no fine tuning or tightening can be done once they are installed.

STUFFING

Otherwise known as "fluff and stuff," the stuffing you choose with which to fill your bear will add to its character. Many bears are under-stuffed with polyester fiberfill, making them feel very huggable, while others are filled with pellets and feel squishy. Still, others are crunchy and hard, giving them an antique look and feel. These bears are usually stuffed with excelsior, or wood wool.

There are many types of stuffing currently available that can be used to stuff a teddy bear, including polyester and acrylic fibers, plastic pellets and glass beads, kapok, and excelsior (wood wool).

Polyester and Acrylic Fibers

These stuffings are readily available at craft, department, and fabric shops. Different types will give the teddy bear various amounts of firmness, allowing for different levels of "huggability." These fibers are clean, easy to use, and inexpensive.

Plastic Pellets and Glass Beads

For floppy bears with added weight, pellets and beads fit the bill, although they can be somewhat messy to use. They are available at most craft stores in the doll making supply department. Plastic pellets are also available in a scented version for a sweet-smelling teddy.

Kapok

Generally found in antique bears, kapok is a soft, silky fiber from a tropical tree's seed pod. Bears stuffed with kapok generally feel quite firm.

Excelsior

Also known as wood wool, excelsior is found extensively in antique and old bears and is still used by some manufacturers today. A funnel is used to place the stuffing inside the bear. Bears stuffed with excelsior feel crunchy and hard. Excelsior can be found in teddy bear supply shops.

PAWS

A variety of different looks can be achieved by making your teddy bear's paws from various fabrics, felts, leathers, or ultrasuede. For real fur bears, the coat's lining can add to the vintage look when used as paw material. Paws can be embroidered, painted, or covered with lace. A little imagination can go a long way here!

Leather can be used for paw and foot pads. Here is a small sampling of the many types available.

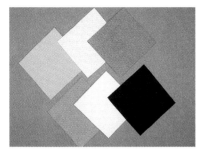

Ultrasuede is a fine quality faux suede. It comes in many colors and makes beautiful paw pads.

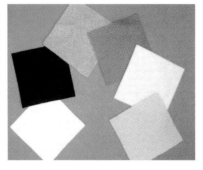

Felt, which is available in many colors, can be used for your teddy's paw pads. Felt was the most common paw material in bears made early in the twentieth century.

Lining from fur coats can add a touch of vintage elegance to your real fur teddy bear. Many linings are beautifully embossed and embroidered.

Many linings are beautiful—on both sides.

INSERTS

Inserts like music boxes and squeakers can add special charm to your bear. You can also insert a "time capsule" to commemorate a special event or pose your bear in various positions by using armatures.

Music Boxes

Music boxes are fairly simple to install and can add a very personalized touch, such as a favorite melody, to your bear. Music boxes that require a grommet and an installation tool can be purchased at fabric stores. See Project 5, Charlotte O'Bear on page 92, for installation instructions. Flat electronic music boxes that do not require a key are also available.

Growlers and Squeakers

Growlers make a bear roar when it is tipped. By using two growlers taped together, the bear will growl when tipped in either direction. Squeakers will have your bear making noise when its belly is pressed. They are installed by simply placing them in the bear's belly. A muslin casing can be sewn to cover them to prevent "friction" wear from the stuffing and to keep the stuffing from getting inside.

Time Capsule

A small plastic container, such as a 35mm film canister, inserted into a bear can make a special memory keeper. Use one for a snip from a baby's first haircut or a special picture of the bear maker and the bear's recipient.

Armatures

Look at a teddy bear supply shop for several types of wired and posable armatures. When attached to your bear's joints, the teddy can be posed into many whimsical positions. Installation difficulty varies with the different types of armatures used. See the manufacturer's instructions for installing them.

Want to make your bear growl or play a special song? There are many types of inserts you can use!

Chapter 2

Fur Coats 101

Fur Coats 101

This chapter is intended to be an introduction to fur, so even if you have never worked with real fur before, don't worry. First, there is a brief glossary of terms to help you understand key terminology covered in this chapter, followed by a listing of some of the most common furs used to make bears. The listing is given in order of "popularity," based on the orders I receive.

Glossary of "Fur Talk"

Black lining: A cotton lining sewn by hand directly to the pelts of a coat, which gives the coat additional strength and durability.

Guard hairs: The long, coarse hairs that are the most visible portion of the fur.

Leather (Animal hide): The underside of an animal's fur.

Pelt seams: The seams where individual pelts have been joined by a special sewing machine to make a coat.

Pelted coat: A term used for coats that have (1- to 4-inch) strips of fur separated by strips of leather.

Pelts (Skins): The individual skins used to make a coat. Some coats, such as mink, are made up of hundreds of small skins. Large animals, such as mouton lamb, have large pelts; hence the coat is made of only a few skins.

Undercoat (Under fur): The short, soft, downy fur that makes up the most dense portion of a fur. It will often be a different color than the longer guard hairs.

IDENTIFYING FUR

Is there a teddy bear hiding in your old fur coat? Few teddy bears exist that have the appeal and sentimental attraction, not to mention the luxury, as a genuine fur bear. You'll want to have these charming creatures tucked in with you on a cold winter's night; nothing can compare to the silky splendor of these teddies.

Fur coats abound in many sizes, styles, and colors. Knowing the species of your coat will help you determine the best design and size of bear to make. Virtually all types of fur can be used to make one or more of the patterns in this book. The following is a listing of some furs that can be used for bear making. See page 22 for a chart summarizing this information.

MINK

Red mink coat.

Mink is a true luxury fur. It is soft and downy with a slightly longer guard hair, yet the fur is quite short. Common colors include tan, brown, bone, red, gray, and black. Mink is by far the most popular fur coat in North America. It works well for virtually all sizes of bears. Mink is easy to sew; however, because often a large number of pelts is used per coat, the teddy pattern pieces must be well lined. A coat made from mink paws or heads will have a lot of little pieces with the pelt seams clearly visible on the right side of the fur. Mink head and the similar mink paw can be made into bears but these seam lines will show on your finished bear.

MUSKRAT

Muskrat coat.

Muskrat is a medium-length fur with a soft down undercoat and long shiny guard hairs. It comes in many shades, ranging from bone to dark brown. In the natural shades, it will have a gray undercoat. Muskrat pelts range in size from small to medium and are easy to sew. This fur works best with bears 10 to 24 inches tall.

SEAL

Seal coat.

Seal fur is short and usually black in color, with an extremely soft texture. The length of the fur makes seal work the best for bears in the 7- to 17-inch height range. The pelts are a medium size and easy to sew.

I made this teddy from a seal coat. I used the lining for the paws and bow; notice how I incorporated the monograms on the bow.

All Because of a Hat

Imagine a man returning to England after several years of exploration in the New World. He is wearing a beaver pelt robe, sewn by the native inhabitants of the land which he purchased for several trinkets of silver. He is, in fact, wearing the robe with the fur on the inside for warmth! The guard hairs have been worn off and the fur has been polished to a rich glossy sheen.

Upon his arrival home, the robe is purchased right off his back by another man of notable status who is a hat maker by trade. He has never seen such beautiful glossy beaver pelts as those which make up the coat. When it was learned that this new type of beaver was a plentiful little creature, the fur trade was launched.

Beaver fur was unique in that the under fur had tiny hooks which made a superior grade of felt for hats. In addition, it was dark, shiny, lightweight, and best of all, waterproof—it was the perfect hat material. From the 1600s until the late 1880s, the well-adorned head of every fashionable European gentleman was topped with a "beaver," as they were known. Hats also bore such illustrious names as The Continental, The Wellington, and The D'Orsay. Men were not alone in their finery; women and children wore beaver muffs for warming icy fingers, as well as beaver collars, hats, and capes.

For the next 150 years, the dam-building rodent with the paddle-like tail influenced the history of a continent. The fur business was competitive and ruthless and grew to produce such commercial giants as the Hudson Bay Company, the Northwest Company, and Jacob Astor's Great American Fur Company. Fur trading posts were established in a wide belt across the middle of North America, and this area became a hub of activity. "Voyageurs" traveled from Montreal to the forts in birch bark canoes loaded with trade goods. Meanwhile, native traders and trappers taught the Europeans how to live in the new, wild country by providing knowledge of such essentials as snowshoes and medicinal herbs.

"Pierre Bear" Voyageur Extraordinaire is dressed in an authentic belt with willow snow shoes. Pierre is 15 inches tall and made from synthetic plush using the Classic Ted pattern with the short muzzle (see page 64).

Eventually, the beaver became scarce and the silk hat more fashionable. The fur trade, however, did not die; it merely shifted its focus. Conservation areas were established and commercial fur ranching was introduced. By the 1920s and '30s, motion pictures began to influence the fashion scene and photogenic furs such as fox became highly desirable, and cosmopolitan women draped tiny red fox pelts with lifelike teeth and glass eyes over their coats.

To revisit the heyday of the fur trading era, one can take a trip to Old Fort William, located on the banks of the Kaministiqua River in Thunder Bay, Ontario. The Old Fort is rated as one of the top ten destinations in Canada. It is an authentic recreation the Northwest Company's operation from 1803 to 1821, complete with historic characters. Fortunes were made at these forts and the course of history was changed, all for the glorious hat made from the industrious rodent with the buck teeth and impressive fur.

MOUTON

Mouton coat.

Mouton is a very dense pile-like wool; coats made from it are done so with large pelts. The leather is generally black while the fur is chocolate brown. The pelts are very thick, making this type of fur very difficult to work with. Use it only for bears at least 20 inches tall. If you have difficulties identifying it, the weight of the coat may help you because mouton is quite heavy.

RABBIT

Rabbit coats are made with large, thin pelts that are very easy to sew. The fur's length is medium to long and very soft. It does, however, have the tendency to shed. These coats will make bears in all sizes and are an excellent choice for the beginner.

Rabbit coat.

If you are making a bear for the first time, I do not recommend mouton. It is very hard to work with and you may not want to make another bear! Keep this coat for a later project, and work with it as though you were sewing a long fur (see the following page).

BEAVER

Beaver is a medium-length fur with a beautiful, soft texture. It is usually tan or brown with a darker brown shading or stripe running lengthwise through it. The pelts range in size from small to medium and are easy to work with. Beaver also appears in a sheared version which is also very soft to the touch. Gorgeous 10- to 22-inch tall teddy bears can be made with beaver fur.

Beaver coat.

These bears are made from South American Beaver fur. It is different from North American fur in that the leather backing is more pliable and the guard hairs are coarser. These furs are also called Nutri.

PERSIAN LAMB

Persian lamb coat.

Persian lamb was very popular for coats in the 1950s. It is usually black but also comes in gray and brown. The pelts are quite large and can be thick, making this fur somewhat difficult to sew, but pelts in good shape will still be easy to work with. Persian lamb works well for 10- to 20-inch tall bears. Bears larger than 20 inches tall will look thin, but can be balanced if given a fluffy mink or fox stole to wear or a large bow (see Auntie Bear-nadette on page 85).

This Persian lamb teddy bear is one of my favorites. Made from a beautiful gray jacket, she wears the coat's mink collar as a stole, which is fastened with an antique broach. I used the Auntie Bear-nadette pattern (page 85) to make her.

Working with Long Furs

Although they may take a little more time to make, teddy bears created from long furs are undeniably spectacular to hug and admire! You will need to keep a few things in mind when working with long furs.

First, wear a garbage bag! It may not be this year's hottest fashion runway item, but you'll be thankful that you don't have to pluck excess fur from your clothing later. To do this, cut holes in the bottom and slip it over your arms and head.

Second, work with a large pattern. Because of the thickness of the leather and the density of the pelts, small pieces, once sewn, can be very difficult to turn. Here, bigger is better. I recommend starting with the 22-inch Classic Ted pattern or the 17-inch Auntie Bear-nadette (pages 64 and 85, respectively).

Third, always use a leather needle, both for hand and machine sewing. Don't be surprised if you break a few of these as they strike the seams in the pelts while you sew; this is quite common. As a precaution, wear safety glasses to prevent injury. Pay special attention to color matching and pelt lines (see page 27). Long furs usually will have you dealing with one or both of these considerations. Be extra careful when cutting the pattern pieces so you do not cut the fur itself. Take small snips and cut only the leather backing.

Fourth, be sure to tuck the fur into the seams as you sew. Fur trapped between the pattern layers will be difficult to remove later. Finally, because of the thickness of the combined leather and dense fur, you may need to sew a portion of your bear by hand. Have a good thimble handy and use your pliers to pull the needle through the layers should it become stuck.

COYOTE

Coyote coat.

Coyote coats have long, multi-colored fur with leather strips sewn between the pelts. Colors range from white to brown, rust, and black—and all of these colors can be found within a single coat. The fur is coarse and pelts can be thick, making sewing difficult. Use coyote fur for bears 22 inches and taller.

This huggable character is made from a coyote coat.

CURLY LAMB

Curly lamb makes wonderful, fanciful bears when patiently sewn. Pelts are large and soft, but can be thick, and the fur ranges from silky to coarse. Curly lamb is most often found in white, bone, and black shades. It is best used for bears 22 inches and taller.

Curly lamb coat.

RACCOON

Raccoon fur is long and brown with silver, white, and black tips. The fur is coarse, making sewing a little difficult, but the resulting bears are fabulous. Small- to medium-sized pelts make up these coats. Use raccoon for bears more than 18 inches tall.

Raccoon coat.

Fox

Fox is a gorgeous long fur, ranging in color from white to silver, red, or multi-colored. The pelts are soft and easy to sew. Coats are usually assembled with leather strips between the pelts, so choose a coat with wide pelts for the best results. Fox is best for bears 22 inches and taller, although with some patience and hand sewing techniques, you can make a smaller bear.

Silver fox coat.

This teddy bear, Alaska, is made from a silver fox coat. I gave him a dog collar with his name engraved on a pewter tag.

I made this 22-inch bear from a fox jacket.

Fox coat variation.

This alphabetical table includes some fur types not listed on the previous pages (chinchilla, kid marten, sable, and squirrel). I have included them here because you may have coats made of these furs, but photos were not available at press time.

Fur Type	Description	Ease of Sewing	Best for Bears Sized
Beaver	Glossy, medium-length fur. Usually dark brown.	Easy to moderate.	10-22 inches.
Chinchilla	Exceptionally soft, medium-length fur. Bluish-gray.	Moderate. The pelts can be fragile.	10-22 inches.
Coyote	Long fur with coarse guard hairs. Colors vary from white to charcoal gray and are often mixed within one coat.	Difficult due to the length and density of the fur.	22 inches or more.
Curly lamb	Long, curly fur with no guard hairs. Usually white.	Difficult due to the length and sometimes coarse texture.	22 inches or more.
Fox	Soft, dense under fur with long guard hairs. White, silver, black, and red.	Moderate to difficult. The fur's length makes it tedious to sew, but the result is stunning.	22 inches or more.
Kid	Short, curly, or wavy coarse fur. Usually found in gray and white shades.	Easy.	All sizes.
Marten	Ultra-soft, dense under fur with long, glossy guard hairs. Ranges from pale yellow to blue-black.	Easy to moderate.	10-22 inches.
Mink	Short, soft under fur with lustrous guard hairs. Color ranges from pale cream shades to black.	Easy.	All sizes.
Mouton	Short, dense fur on thick pelts. Usually brown. Very heavy.	Very difficult to sew due to the thickness of the pelts and density of the fur.	20 inches and more. Use only for bears with large limbs for ease of turning.
Muskrat	Soft gray under fur with long, silky guard hairs.	Easy to moderate.	10-24 inches.
Persian lamb	Tightly curled, soft wool. Usually black, but also found in gray and brown.	Easy to moderate depending on its age.	10-20 inches.
Rabbit	Soft, short- to medium-length fur. Ranges in color from white to black and is often dyed novelty colors.	Easy. Fur may have a tendency to shed.	All sizes.
Raccoon	Long, sometimes coarse, fur. Pelts can be fairly thick. A mixture of gray, brown, and black.	Difficult due to the thickness of the pelts and length of the fur.	18 inches or more.
Sable	Beautiful, soft, dense fur with long guard hairs. Brown or black.	Easy.	10-20 inches.
Seal	Very soft, short fur. Guard hairs are coarse and generally removed. Usually black.	Easy.	7-17 inches.
Squirrel	Soft fur with long guard hairs. Gray, red, and black are common.	Easy. Can be fragile.	7-17 inches.

DISASSEMBLING A COAT

Before you begin, if your coat has unwanted odors or is very dirty, have it professionally cleaned. The cost is relatively small and your bear will thank you in the end.

Tip

Wear a large lawn or garden garbage bag to keep fur and dust from sticking to your clothes while you work. Simply cut a hole in the bag's bottom, in the middle, for your head, and two holes for your arms on the sides.

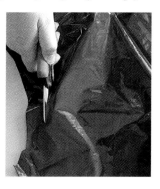

❶ Using a pair of sharp scissors or a seam ripper, unstitch the entire lining and remove it from the coat. Some large hand stitching may be present over the body of the coat that attaches the lining to the coat. Be careful not to tear the pelts when you are removing these stitches. If the coat has an additional black lining sewn directly onto the pelts, do not remove this because it will provide extra strength for your bear.

The inside of a coat with the lining removed.

❷ Open up all hems and facings and remove any interfacing and fillers present. Cut off the pockets and remove all buttons and closures.

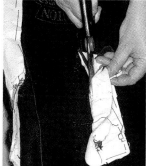 

Cut off the pockets.   *If there is any interfacing, remove it.*

Tip

Wear a dust mask to keep from inhaling dirt and other particles.

❸ Cut around the arm seam, completely removing the arm from the coat. Cut the arm open along the underarm seam so it lies flat. Remove the collar from the coat by cutting the stitching or by cutting the fur along the seam line. Cut open the shoulder seams so the coat itself will lie flat.

❹ Remove all loose threads from the coat and vacuum the raw edges with a crevice tool to remove loose fur. Vacuum the backs of the pelts to remove dust, dirt, and leather which has deteriorated. If you suspect insects or mites may have used your coat for a home, wrap the fur in a plastic bag and place it in a freezer for several days. You could also put several mothballs, which are now available in a cedar scent, in with the coat. To freshen the fur, place it in a dryer on the air fluff cycle with one or two scented fabric softening sheets. Let the cycle run for about ten minutes. Do not use a heat setting on your dryer. Coats can also be hung outside on a clothesline to freshen them.

❺ For very dry pelts, put some liquid glycerin on a rag and rub it over the leather underside of the pelt. Liquid glycerin can be purchased in craft stores in the cake decorating department. This will soften the leather and make it more pliable. Do not use vegetable or other oils because they will seep through your bear and stain its fur and whatever the bear may be sitting on.

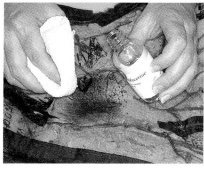

You can soften a dry coat with glycerin.

❻ Disassemble the coat's lining in the same way as the fur portion (Steps 1 to 3). Remove any monograms or tags you would like to keep. Wash the lining in cold water, dry, and press. Linings can be used for decorative bows and paw pads for your bear (see page 16).

Chapter 3

Great Beginnings

Pattern Preparation and Layout

Once you have determined what kind of coat you have, it is time to choose a bear to make from the designs in this book (see Chapter 7). If you are new to bear making, choosing a simple bear for your first project can be a wise decision. Use an inexpensive synthetic fur to get your "paws" wet; this way, you'll feel more confident when cutting into your grandmother's heirloom stole or that $100 piece of mohair later. If you do not have a coat, don't want to use one, or would like to make a practice bear before cutting into your coat, all of the patterns can also be made from synthetic plush or mohair. Copy the one of your liking, being sure to include all of the pattern markings. Enlarge or reduce all of the pattern pieces to the desired size on a photocopier. You may find this formula helpful when altering the size of your pattern:

Size of pattern divided by 10 equals the increments of enlargement or reduction. For example, if the pattern in the book makes a 14-inch bear, divide 14 by 10. This will give you a 1.4 inch increment. For every 10 percent the pattern is enlarged or reduced, the bear's height will change by 1.4 inches. If you want to make a bear about 17 inches tall from this pattern, enlarge the 14-inch bear pattern by 20 percent; your finished bear will be 16.8 inches tall (2 x 1.4). Remember that a larger bear will require more fur or fabric than is stated in the bear's materials list.

With your completed pattern in hand, use a glue stick to glue the pattern to bristol board or stiff cardboard, or use a plastic place mat to make your template; the pattern pieces will last much longer than those made of cardboard. Cut out the pattern pieces. This is the template you can use for as many bears as you want without ruining the original pattern. You will trace around the templates to transfer the pattern onto the fur.

FINDING THE NAP

All fur coats and fur fabrics, including plush and mohair, have a nap. The nap is simply the direction in which the fur travels. Run your hand over the fur to determine the nap. The fur will feel smooth under your hand when you are running with the nap.

Checking for your fur's nap is easy and essential.

When you are making a bear, the pattern pieces should be placed so that the arrow runs in the same direction as the nap. This will ensure that your finished bear will have its fur running down, just like animals in the wild.

Some coats, such as seal, sheared beaver, and mouton, are sewn with the nap, or fur, running up the length of the coat. This was done to make the coat glisten in the light and highlight the fur. You will need to turn these coats upside down before laying out your pattern.

A bad hair day! Make sure the direction of the nap corresponds to the direction of the arrows on the pattern!

Synthetic plush will always have a visible nap, running with the grain of the knit backing. Mohair comes in an enormous variety of textures. It can be wavy, curly, distressed, and feathered, and these qualities can make the nap difficult to determine. Use your best judgment, because mohair can be "trained" in some spots on your finished teddy to go where you want it (see page 126).

PATTERN LAYOUT

Choose a marking pen that will easily be seen on your coat or fabric. If the inside of your coat is dark leather, or if your fabric is black, choose a gold or silver marker for the best results. For light-colored coat interiors and fabrics, black ink or a marker will work well.

Trace around the templates on the back of the fabric or leather inside of the coat, transferring all of the pattern markings. Pattern pieces that say "reverse one" mean you will need to trace around the template and then flip it over and trace around it again. Place the pattern pieces as close together as possible to conserve your material. Real fur may require a bit more material because you will have to take color matching and pelt lines into consideration.

I made these plastic templates from old, inexpensive plastic place mats found at yard sales!

Trace around the template onto the leather (the back of the fur).

Matching Colors and Pelt Lines

Laying out a pattern on a fur coat will require some special consideration. Many fur coats have obvious changes in color throughout the fur. When cutting out a pattern piece such as the head, it is necessary to match the colors on both sides of the head. If a dark stripe runs through the middle of the right side of the head, position the left side of the head on the fur so that a dark stripe also runs through the middle of the left side. By doing this, you will ensure that your finished teddy looks balanced and appealing.

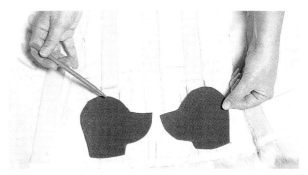

Be sure to match pelt lines if your coat has them. This will help your finished bear look more symmetrical.

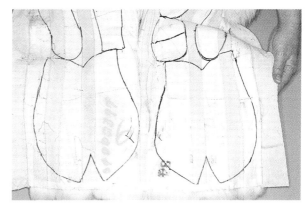

Careful pattern layout is required on pelted coats.

Color matching is important in helping you achieve a symmetrical and aesthetically pleasing bear.

You must also consider the leather and bias tape strips sewn between the pelts in the coat. These give dimension to the coat, but can make your bear look striped. Try to avoid these strips in the head area, but if this is not possible, be sure all of the strips are symmetrically placed on all of the pattern pieces.

The inside of a pelted coat.

Careful pattern placement is essential when working with pelted coats; avoid the "mummy" look!

CUTTING

You can use the same technique for cutting out pattern pieces, regardless of whether you are using fabric or genuine fur. With small, sharp scissors, lift up on the backing with the tip of the scissors while gently pushing the fur down. Take short, small snips. Cut only the backing and not the fur itself. Cutting the fur will result in "flat" spots wherever there is a incision, usually at the seams. By snipping only the backing, be it knitted, woven, or leather, your teddy will have a uniformly fluffy coat.

Use caution when snipping the fur's backing (be it woven, knitted, or leather). Avoid cutting the fur itself; fur that is cut will result in "flat spots" at the bear's seams.

When all of the parts have been cut out, vacuum around the edges with a crevice tool to remove loose fur, both real and faux. Be careful here! Hang onto the pieces tightly so they don't disappear into the vacuum cleaner. Also, vacuum the remnants of the coat or the fur fabric to keep your work area tidy. More bears can be made later from the remnants, or the scraps can be used for projects (see page 120).

LINING

This step is *crucial* if you are making a real fur bear. Unlined, teddies will split where the pelts are sewn together. Tears will also occur if the pelts are weak or dry. Without a lining, your bear may fall apart when stuffed! (Omit this step if you are working with mohair or synthetic plush.)

Cut a second bear from unbleached cotton muslin. This will be your lining. Use a glue stick or spray adhesive and *lightly* apply glue to the lining. Glue the lining to the corresponding fur piece. If you already have a black lining attached to your coat, glue any loose edges down first, and then apply the cotton muslin lining over the top of the

O no! Here I go! Hang onto your pattern pieces when vacuuming them to avoid having them disappear into the machine.

black lining. The black lining by itself will not adequately protect your pelts. Use only enough glue to hold the lining in place. Once you begin sewing, the stitching will hold the muslin more securely. Too much glue may cause problems with your sewing machine needle by making it sticky and tacky. Trim any muslin lining so it matches the raw edges of your fur pieces.

Cut paw pads from the desired fabric or ultrasuede. If you are using the coat's satin lining for the pads, I recommend cutting a second set from an iron-on interfacing. Iron it on according to the manufacturer's instructions before sewing. This fusible interfacing helps prevent the edges from fraying and provides stability.

You are now ready to begin sewing.

$\mathcal{L}$ining a real fur bear is crucial to avoid tears and stuffing explosions later!

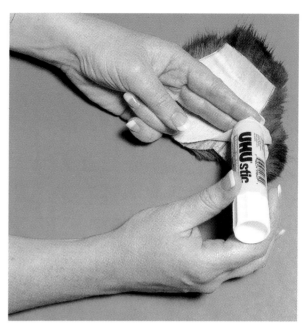

Glue the lining to the back of the fur pieces with a glue stick.

Remember to cut a second bear from cotton muslin.

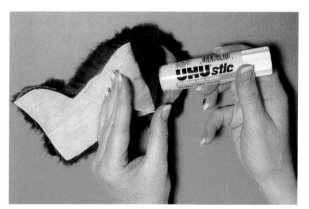

Make sure to glue down any black lining already attached to the coat.

Chapter 4

Sewing the Teddy

Sewing the Teddy

In this chapter, you will learn how the pattern pieces are sewn together and the basic hand stitches required (for some piecing, the sewing cannot be done by machine). The instructions included apply to all of the projects in Chapter 7 (although any special instructions will be listed at the beginning of each project.)

Tools

I am often asked if I use a special machine to sew my bears. I don't; I use a five-stitch machine that has been around for many years. You don't need fancy sewing machines to make teddy bears. All of the bears in this book can even be sewn by hand using a backstitch if you don't have access to a sewing machine. Gather up these things:

- Leather needle (also called a glover) if you are using real fur
- Leather needle for your machine if you are using real fur
- All-purpose needle for your machine if you are using mohair and synthetics
- Various sizes of all-purpose needles for hand sewing mohair and synthetics
- Straight pins or pinning alternatives (see page 33)
- Heavy-duty thread

SAMPLE HAND STITCHES

Sewing a part or all of your bear by hand may seem tedious, but the results can be very pleasing and worth the effort. When sewing by hand, you will find there is less shifting of the fur or fabric, which results in a neater finished bear. I sew all of my bears' faces by hand using a backstitch to ensure they are nice and straight. Similarly, I find I can match foot pads to one another better if I sew them in by hand.

Besides the backstitch, running, whip, and ladder stitches are also important to bear making and are described in more detail on the following page.

Whip Stitch

Use this for tacking pattern pieces into place and holding them temporarily until more permanent sewing has been completed.

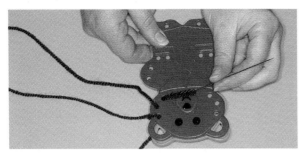

A whip stitch is used to tack pieces into place before sewing them more permanently.

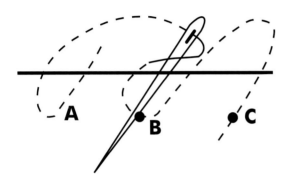

1 In and out at A.

2 Now, in and out at B.

3 Proceed to C, etc.

Backstitch

The entire bear can be sewn using a backstitch. I recommend using it for the face and paw pads because it produces a more even finish than the machine does.

1 In at A.

2 Out at B.

3 Back in at A, out at C.

4 Back in at B, out at D, etc.

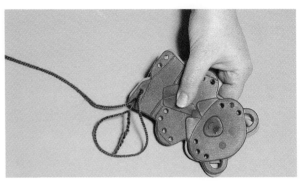

I use a backstitch for sewing the gusset to the head and sewing on the paw pads. If you don't have a sewing machine, the entire bear can be sewn using this stitch.

Ladder Stitch

Use this stitch for closing seams.

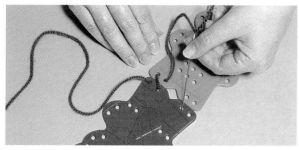

A ladder stitch is used for sewing the bear's seams after it is stuffed.

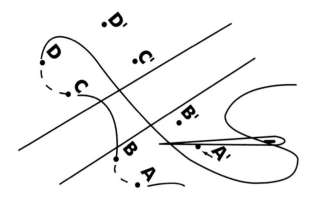

1 In at A, out at B.

2 In at C, out at D.

3 In at A', out at B'.

4 In at C', out at D'.

Running Stitch

You can use this stitch for gathering the bear's neck opening.

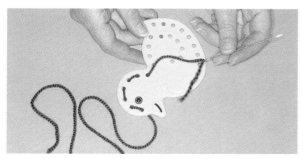

A running stitch can be used when gathering the bear's neck opening before jointing it to the body as described in Chapter 6.

PINNING ALTERNATIVES

Occasionally, you may find it difficult to pin pattern pieces together, especially if you are working with very long fur or a thick leather backing. There are several alternatives to pins that work well.

Paper Clips

These are remarkable for holding pattern pieces together and are very useful for people with arthritis. Use heavy-duty metal clips for thicker fabrics. Remove the clips as you sew.

You can paper-clip pieces together.

Tape

Scotch tape works well for real fur pattern pieces. You can sew over the tape and remove it after stitching. Masking tape will also do the job.

Taping pieces together works because it will hold the pieces firmly and you can sew right over the tape!

Staples

Another useful way to hold the pieces together is to staple them. This method works best for mohair and synthetics (I do not recommend stapling real fur because the staples may tear the leather). Use care when removing the staples (with a staple remover) so you do not tear the fabric backing.

If you are in a bind, you can staple pieces together, but be careful to remove them all when finished because they are not very cuddly! Also be careful that you do not tear the fabric's or fur's backing when removing them.

SEWING

Here are some guidelines for sewing your bear.

1 Use a 1/4-inch seam allowance for all of your sewing unless otherwise stated.

2 If you would like your bear to be more durable, zigzag along the seam allowance for reinforcement.

3 All seams are sewn with the right, or fur, sides together unless otherwise stated.

4 Always pin your pieces together before sewing because the fur will tend to shift during sewing.

5 Make sure that all pattern markings, especially the joint makings, have been transferred to the fur, or muslin lining if you are making a real fur bear, before you begin sewing.

~~~~~~~ *Tip* ~~~~~~~

For the best results, tuck the fur into the seams as you sew. This will give you a uniformly fluffy bear with no fur trapped between the stitching.

The Body

1 Fold each body piece in half and stitch along the stitch lines marked at the top and bottom.

Fold the body and sew at the top and bottom.

2 Place both halves together, matching the top and bottom seams. Be sure to have the front side markings together. Pin the pieces together. Sew around the body, leaving a 1/8-inch opening at the top, as shown in the pattern markings; this is where the head joint will later be inserted. Also leave an opening at the back for stuffing, as shown.

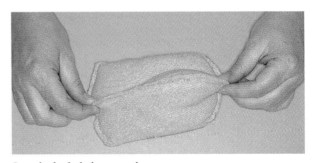

Sew the body halves together.

Arms

1 Pin the paw pads, if applicable, to the inner arm pieces. Place the inner arm against the outer arm, right sides together, to ensure that the shapes match. If they do not, switch the paw pads because they are not attached to the correct inner arm pieces.

Match the inner arm with the outer.

2 With right sides together, sew the paw pads in place. Match the inner arm to the outer arm. Pin and sew all around, leaving an opening at the back of the arm as marked. Repeat the process for the second arm.

Legs

1 Pin the leg pieces together to make two legs. Sew from the tip of the toe to the tip of the heel, leaving the bottom of the foot open. Also leave an opening at the back of the leg, as shown on the pattern.

2 Using a whip stitch, tack the paw pad onto the bottom of the foot at the toe and heel. Pin the paw pad in place. Using doubled heavy-duty thread and a backstitch, sew the footpad around the foot opening, maintaining a 1/4-inch seam allowance. All stitches should be 1/8 inch to 1/4 inch long. Pull each stitch tight so the stitching won't show later when the bear is stuffed. Repeat the process for the second leg.

The Head

1 Pin the head pieces together from the tip of the nose to the base of the neck. Sew the pieces together.

2 Using a whip stitch, tack the center nose portion of the gusset into the seam of the head at the tip of the nose.

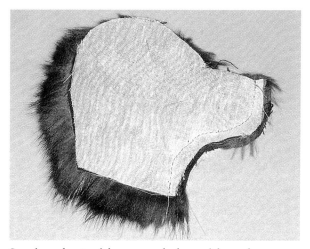

Sew from the tip of the nose to the base of the neck.

3 Pin the right and left sides of the gusset to the corresponding sides of the head.

Tack the gusset at the seam.

Take a little extra time to ensure that all parts are pinned evenly and straight; a crooked head cannot be disguised later. Sewing the gusset by hand minimizes shifting of the fur, be it real or faux.

4 Using a backstitch and doubled heavy-duty thread, sew the gusset in place.

Ears

1 Pin the ears, right sides together.

2 Sew around each ear, leaving the bottom edge open.

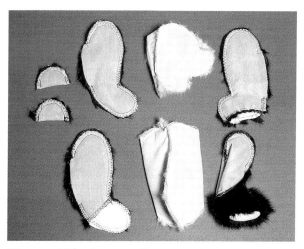

Way to go! The pieces are all sewn together!

Finishing

Turn the teddy bear parts right side out and admire your handiwork! In the next chapters, you will see your bear come to life.

Chapter 5

Adding Personality

Adding Personality

Creating the Perfect Face

The popular saying "the eyes are the window of the soul" is true even for a teddy bear. You are now about to begin one of the most enjoyable parts of bear making: creating the face. It is very important that you take your time with these steps so that your teddy will be perfect. Time spent paying attention to details now will be well worth the effort when your finished bear tilts its head and smiles at you later. So, gather up your bear making tools, including those listed below, and watch as your teddy becomes an individual little character!

Tools

- Small, sharp scissors for cutting and shaping the fur
- 6-inch soft sculpture needle for inserting glass eyes
- 2- to 3-inch leather needle for hand sewing if you are using real fur
- Needle nose pliers
- Stuffing stick (if you don't have one, a chopstick or the end of a wooden spoon will work)
- Optional: Thimble
- Optional: Liquid tacky glue
- Black magic marker
- Optional: Electric shaver or dog grooming tool
- All-purpose thread

Materials

Before you begin assembly, you must choose the types of eyes and nose you want to use. Plastic safety eyes and noses are inserted *before* stuffing, and glass eyes and embroidered and leather noses are applied *after* stuffing. Some of the additional materials you will need in this section are:

- Heavy-duty or carpet thread
- Stuffing
- Pearl cotton to embroider the nose or a plastic safety nose
- Pair of plastic safety, glass, or shoe button eyes

INSTALLING SAFETY EYES

1 Turn your bear's head inside out. Check to make sure the eye placement markings are straight and that one eye is not higher than the other. Sometimes as the fur shifts while you are sewing, these markings can become misaligned and the result will be a distorted face.

2 You could change the position of the eyes at this point, but keep in mind the following as you make your new markings:

🐾 Keep the eyes in line with the bridge of the nose; this is where the gusset has an abrupt change in shape. If you put the eyes higher than this, they will be on the teddy's forehead, and if they are lower, your bear will be perpetually looking up at the ceiling.

🐾 Small eyes, placed close together, give a modern, funky look. Large eyes spaced further apart will make the bear look younger and more innocent.

3 Once you are happy with the eye placement, use an awl to poke small holes through the backing and fur. Insert the pegged portion of the eyes through the holes so that the pegs protrude to the inside (wrong side) of the head. Double-check the placement for proper alignment. Press on the lock washers, flat side down, as far as they will go onto each eye. The eyes are now secure.

Keep the eyes symmetrical and at the bridge of the nose for a more balanced appearance.

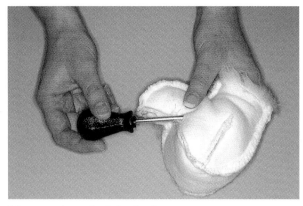

Use an awl to poke holes for the eyes.

Insert the pegged positions into the holes.

Press on the lock washers.

Eye positioning and size can alter your bear's character.

INSTALLING A SAFETY NOSE

A safety nose is installed the same way as safety eyes.

1 Locate the exact center of where the gusset meets the two head pieces at the tip of the muzzle.

2 Trim away 1/8 inch of the seam allowance here on each piece. Using the awl, poke a very small hole where all three seams meet.

3 Insert the nose from the outside (right side) so that the peg protrudes to the inside (wrong side) of the head.

Insert the safety nose into the small hole.

4 Double-check the placement.

5 Press on the lock washer, flat side down, as far as it will go.

Press on the lock washer.

6 Turn the head right side out and admire your work! Using a needle, remove any fur trapped behind the eyes and nose.

THE ART OF STUFFING THE HEAD

Filling your bear's head with fluff is really an exercise in shaping and defining. Teddy bears have been known to gorge on enormous amounts of the puffy stuff, so be careful how much you feed it. (I recommend using polyester fiberfill for stuffing the head because it is clean, easy to use and find, and it is inexpensive.)

1 Take small pieces of stuffing and place them into the muzzle.

2 Fill the larger portion of the head. Always use small pieces of fluff; this way, you won't get a stuffing jam that prevents sections of the head from being filled.

3 With the aid of the stuffing stick, shape the head by sliding more stuffing along the inside of the fabric and into the muzzle. The muzzle should be stuffed firmly so it does not collapse in the future, because many types of stuffing will soften with age. A firm muzzle also makes the perfect canvas for an embroidered nose.

Use a stuffing stick to stuff the teddy's head.

4 Make sure the stuffing is evenly placed around the pegs if you have installed a safety nose or eyes. Doing this will keep these parts from shifting sideways.

5 Extra stuffing can be placed in the cheeks to further shape the head. When you are finished, the head should feel smooth all around with no large under-stuffed wrinkles.

SHAVING THE MUZZLE

A beautifully shaved muzzle can highlight a bear's soulful eyes and accentuate a pouty mouth. I have, however, encountered many students who were afraid to do this step. After all, once the fur comes off, you can't replace it, and no one wants to ruin a bear after all of the love that has gone into its making.

To take the fear out of shaving the muzzle, start by gathering several small pieces of scrap fur. Using small, sharp scissors, cut the fur to various lengths. Many genuine furs have a different color in the underfur (which can also be very soft and downy). Now practice cutting on a larger piece and try to get a smooth even finish. Practice on scraps until you feel comfortable with the shaving process. You may also like to try the electric shaver, but go slowly with it because it tends to cut the fur quickly.

Clipping the bear's muzzle with scissors.

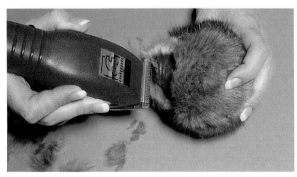

Go slowly if you are going to shave the bear's muzzle with an electric shaver.

> ## Tip
> When shaving the fur, be sure to try for an even finish. Fur that is left too long in places can cause the bear's face to look distorted and disheveled.

If you are certain your bear's muzzle has been cut from a piece of the coat that has no pelt lines in it, go ahead and shave the fur all the way down to the leather if you like. If there are pelt lines, try to leave a little fur (1/8 inch) to hide them.

There are several techniques you can try:

1 Shave the entire muzzle.
- Cut off the top portion of a paper cup.
- Place the bottom of the cup over the bear's muzzle.
- Using the small, sharp scissors, trim the fur all around the edge of the cup, creating a well-defined line.
- Remove all of the fur on the muzzle inside the line you made.
- Remove a little extra fur just around the eyes if necessary.

2 Highlight the eyes and mouth.
- Using the small, sharp scissors, cut a line straight across the forehead, between the eyes.
- Remove all of the fur on the top of the gusset only, staying inside the seams.
- Also remove a rectangle of fur immediately below the nose, around the mouth.

3 Shave the fur to different lengths.
- First, use the paper cup method (Type 1) to create the well-defined circle on the muzzle.
- Now, use the highlighting method (Type 2) and remove the fur on the muzzle and below the nose.
- For the remaining fur, remove only the guard hairs, or just trim off a small portion of the fur.

> ## Tip
> Sometimes I shave the muzzle section of the gusset before I sew the bear's head! This can make sewing easier and can take some of the fear out of the shaving process. If I'm unsure about shaving at any point, I practice, practice, practice on my scraps!

EMBROIDERED NOSES

Use pearl cotton, in any color you'd like, to embroider your bear's nose. Avoid embroidery floss because it will separate as you sew and cause knots and other bumpy, messy problems. A very small dab of glue, under your stitching before you sew, will help keep each stitch tidy and where you want it. You might also try cutting some templates from scraps of felt and holding these to the nose area so that you can see which shape best suits your bear. Here are a few templates to help you get started.

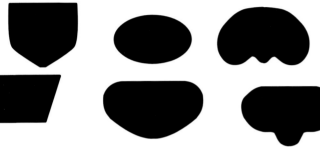

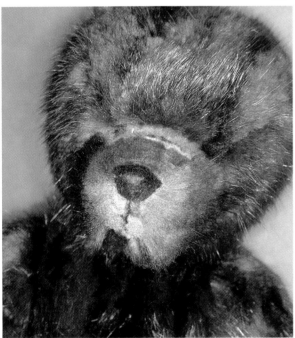

I glued a felt template to the bear so I could see if it suited the bear. I shaved the muzzle using Type 2 on the previous page.

---

❶ Cut the fur very short on the muzzle where the nose will go.

❷ Choose a template and very, very lightly trace around it with a fine pen or air erasing marker, or glue down a felt template.

❸ Using Scotch tape, tape back all the fur around the nose so it doesn't get caught up with the cotton as you are sewing.

❹ Insert the needle at the bottom of the nose, leaving about a 10-inch tail of thread, and exit at the top left corner of the nose.

❺ Make horizontal stitches that lay neatly side by side until you reach the nose bottom. Once again, exit at the top left of the nose.

❻ Now make vertical stitches side by side, filling in the shape of the template.

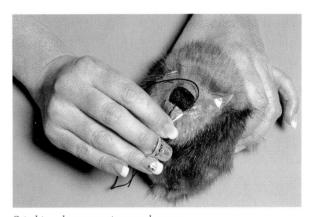

Stitching the nose using pearl cotton.

❼ The final stitch should end where you started, in the middle of the nose's bottom.

❽ Twist the initial tail of thread and the remaining thread together three or four times.

Tip

Cut a template from felt the same color as the pearl cotton you are using. Glue this to the bear's muzzle to form a base and embroider vertical stitches over your template. Any color that shows through the stitching will be the same color as the cotton!

9 Now separate the two into the bear's mouth or smile.

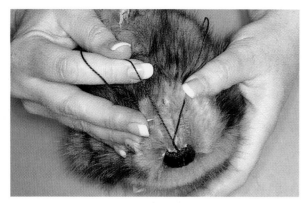

Separate two strands for the mouth.

10 Secure each end separately to the head with a stitch. Knot off the thread ends and bury them into the head and trim.

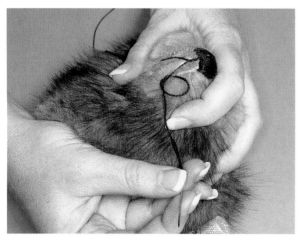

Finally, knot off the ends and hide any remaining pearl cotton by taking a stitch into the bear's head. Exit several inches from the mouth and cut the strand off, close to the head.

Tip

If you have not used a felt template under your stitches, little pieces of fur may insist on popping out between the nose stitches. Cut these off as close to the nose as possible and then color them with a felt marker the same color as the nose. The fur will not only be invisible, but it will also lie flat.

LEATHER NOSES

Leather is a wonderful way to add a touch of character to your bear, especially if you want it to have a really big nose. Cut a small scrap of leather in the color of your choice to a shape similar to the template shown. You can make it larger or smaller as required for your particular bear.

Leather noses can add a real touch of character to your bear. Because they are handmade, each one will look different.

1 Using a backstitch and a 1/8-inch seam allowance, close the darts on either side.

2 Starting at the bottom center, sew the nose to the bear using a whip stitch or small ladder stitch.

3 Tack the top and sides in place with a pin or tiny stitch to keep the nose centered.

4 Place a small wad of stuffing in the nose as you sew to help it retain its shape. If the leather you are using is thin, the edges can be rolled under for a more finished look.

This bear has a handmade leather nose.

ADDING A MOUTH TO PLASTIC AND LEATHER NOSES

You can make your bear happy or sad, grumpy or youthful; all it takes are a few carefully placed stitches!

1 For a plastic nose, cut a piece of pearl cotton about 18 inches long.

2 Wrap it over and behind the safety nose and twist the ends together several times at the bottom.

Twist the ends together.

3 Separate the strands into a smile and secure each end with a stitch to the bear. Bury the thread ends into the bear.

Separate the strands.

4 Use the same method for a leather nose, but secure the strand to the bear at the bottom center of the leather with a single stitch into the bear.

MOUTH STITCH

You might also embroider the mouth using several long stitches to create a more pronounced smile. Follow the stitch placement in this illustration.

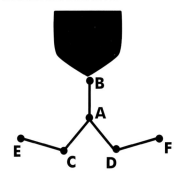

1 Use a long piece of pearl cotton and enter the head from the back, exiting at A.

2 Go in at B and exit at C.

3 Go in at A and exit at D; go in at A and exit at E.

4 Go in at C and exit at F.

5 Go in at D and exit at the back of the head.

6 Secure the loose ends with a stitch or a knot and bury thread ends into the head.

USING GLASS OR SHOE BUTTON EYES

If you are not planning on giving the bear to a child, glass eyes can add an extra sparkle that simply cannot be achieved with plastic. Antique shoe buttons also have a distinctive look and can be very nice if you are making bears like Classic Ted or Auntie Bear-nadette (pages 64 and 85, respectively).

1 To install these eyes, locate the center tip of the muzzle as a point of reference. You may wish to trim the fur slightly here if you have not already done so to help you see what you are doing.

2 Mark the point on one side of the face where you want to position the eye using a pin with a bead on the end. Make sure that it is in line horizontally with the bridge of the muzzle. Remember: too high or too low will look unnatural. Again, you may wish to trim some of the fur around the eye mark.

3 Repeat the process on the other side.

4 Now measure the distance each mark is from the gusset seams and be sure they are the same.

5 Using the awl, poke holes through these markings on an angle toward the opposite ear.

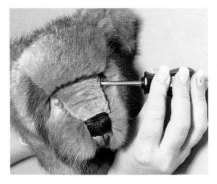

Use an awl to poke holes for the eyes.

6 Double a long piece of heavy-duty thread onto the 6-inch needle and knot the ends. Insert the needle at the gusset seam on top of the right side of the head and exit through the left eye socket. Sounds cruel, but believe me, the teddy won't feel a thing!

7 Sew through the wire loop on the back of the eye and pinch it shut with the pliers. The loops at the back of shoe buttons should not be pinched.

8 Re-enter the left eye hole and pull the eye into position. Place a small dab of tacky glue behind the eye to help secure it.

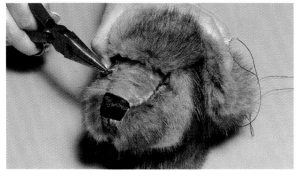

Use pliers to pinch the wire loop shut.

9 Exit at the top of the head where you started. Secure the thread at this point by making a small stitch and tying a knot. The knot will be hidden by the teddy's ear.

10 Once again, enter the head at this same point and cross to the opposite gusset seam where the left ear is.

11 Repeat this entire process to insert the other eye.

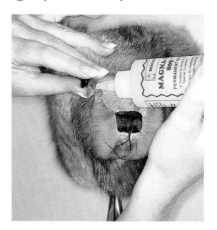

Put a dab of glue behind glass eyes to help keep them in place.

12 When both eyes are in place, direct the needle from the finishing point to the bottom of the neck.

13 Secure the thread with a small stitch and tie a knot.

Tip

A new product called True Eyes is available that allows you to pin various sizes of glass eyes onto your bear in order to find your favorite position. They are then removed and the actual eyes installed. Look for them in teddy bear supply shops.

14 Bury any remaining thread into the head.

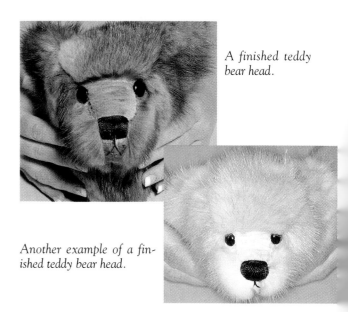

A finished teddy bear head.

Another example of a finished teddy bear head.

The Art of Soft Sculpture

Have you ever wondered how that beautiful teddy bear or cloth doll you saw got its wonderful expression? It was probably the result of a few carefully placed invisible stitches known as soft sculpture. It could be defined as the art of manipulating a stuffed form into a desired shape, but I call it a "little nip here and a little tuck there." One of the most common places in a teddy bear to use soft sculpture is around the eyes. It will work best if you are using glass eyes (but is optional). (I used soft sculpture at the eye sockets on Mulligan, shown on the title page.)

Thread a long needle (also known as a soft sculpture needle) with heavy-duty thread. Start at one eye socket and exit at the other. Place the needle back into the exact spot you just exited and return to your starting point. Try to take all of your stitches through the same entry and exit points so the stitches are invisible on the outside of the bear. After each stitch, pull the thread tight. It will catch on the stuffing in-side the head, and each stitch will draw the eyes in toward one another. You could use the same technique to draw the eyes inward by exiting each stitch at the back of the head.

Soft sculpture can also define your muzzle by accentuating its shape. To do this, stitch from one side to the other along the gusset seams. Always re-enter your exit hole, but make each new exit hole a little lower along the muzzle until you have sculptured along the entire length.

One more place to try this technique is on the bear's paw pads to add definition to the pads.

When you use soft sculpture on a real fur bear, be gentle as you pull the thread taut. Remember that these pelts may be fragile and will not accept the kind of stress that a synthetic or mohair fabric does. I do not recommend sculpting on very old or dry pelts.

Use your imagination and have fun designing your teddy bear's features with soft sculpture!

ATTACHING THE EARS

Before you sew the ears onto the bear, try pinning them in different positions to see how they alter your bear's appearance. The most common or natural look is with the top corner of the ear starting where the gusset meets the head, and with the ear centered on the head if you are looking at its profile.

Use a whip stitch to attach the bear's ears.

❶ To secure the ear while you sew, push long straight pins through the ear and into the head and tack each corner with a small stitch, or use diaper pins to hold the ears in place.

❷ Fold an ear forward on the head.

❸ Using heavy-duty thread, secure the top corner of the ear.

❹ Use about ten whip stitches along the back of the ear to fasten it to the head.

❺ Now, flip the ear over so it is folded down toward the back.

❻ Repeat the whip stitches along the front of the ear. Try to keep all of your stitches small and close to the ear itself. Each stitch should go through both layers of the bear's ears and the head. If you have trouble pulling the needle through, use a pair of pliers to help you.

❼ When you begin the second ear, check its placement every two or three stitches to be sure it matches that of the first ear. Fur tends to slip as you sew, and it is not uncommon for the second ear to shift into an entirely different spot from the first.

Although you may be tempted to skip stitches here, don't! Most people will want to admire your finished bear, and many will pick it up by the ears!

Chapter 6

Putting It All Together

Putting It All Together

Assembling the Teddy

You are now on the homestretch of the bear-making process! In a few short steps, your teddy will be ready for its new home. I often ask my students at the beginning of a workshop if they are planning on giving their bears away as gifts, and about half of the class signed up with those intentions. When we get to this stage, I ask again. By now, most of the students have decided that their first bear must stay home with them! They simply couldn't bear to part with them!

How you choose to stuff your bear will add its final character. It can be firm and substantial, or extra soft and cuddly. There are no rules here, so be guided by your heart. Speaking of heart, you may want to insert a plastic or metal one into your bear before you stitch it shut!

The steps in this chapter will give you a wonderful sense of accomplishment as you watch your work being assembled into a lovable finished teddy bear. There are a few tools you will need for assembly:

- Needle nose pliers for turning cotter pins
- Awl or pointy pair of scissors for poking holes
- Joints of your choice and tools to install them
- Stuffing of your choice
- Stuffing stick or a wooden spoon or chopstick to get stuffing in hard-to-reach places
- Needles or leather needles (if using real fur)
- Heavy-duty thread for sewing the seams
- Felt marker or pen for repositioning the joint markings

JOINTS

Before beginning, you will need to choose the type of joint system you would like to use in your bear. Use the following information, and that in Chapter 1, to help you decide (see the chart on page 51 for a summary of this information).

Plastic Safety Joints

❶ Place the plastic washer over the peg inside the body. Follow this with the lock washer.

❷ With the flat side down, press the washer down onto the peg as far as it will go.

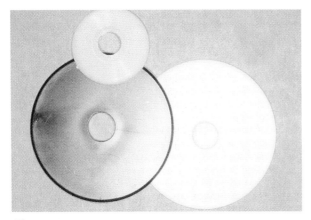

Plastic joints.

Cotter Pin Joints

❶ Place a metal washer, followed by a disk and another metal washer, over the pin inside the body.

❷ Using a needle nose pliers or cotter key, curl each side of the cotter pin tightly down against the metal washer.

Cotter pin joint.

Double Cotter Pin Joints

A On the first cotter pin, place a metal washer, then a hardboard or fiberboard disk, followed by another metal washer.

❷ Curl the cotter pin down tightly against the metal washer.

❸ Slip a second cotter pin through the head of the first so that they dangle from one another. The first pin and disk set is inserted into the head, while the second is installed into the neck opening.

❹ Inside the body, cover the pin with a metal washer, a disk, and a second metal washer in that order.

❺ Curl the cotter pin ends down tightly with the needle nose pliers. When the bear is stuffed, the teddy's head will wobble around quite loosely.

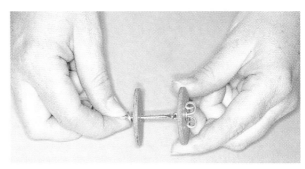

A double cotter pin can be used if you want a wobbly head or arms and legs. They give your teddy that "well-loved over the years" look.

Installing double cotter joints.

Tip

It is very important to use the correct size of joint in your assembly. Use the largest size of disk that will fit into the arms or legs. Joints that are too large won't fit into the arms or legs, and the arms and legs will be extremely loose if the disks are too small—it may not even be able to sit up! Joints that are too small also contribute to "football" shoulders, those that "hump" above the bear's chin level.

③ Using the ratchet, turn the lock nut until the desired tightness has been reached.

④ Check all joints to ensure even tightness.

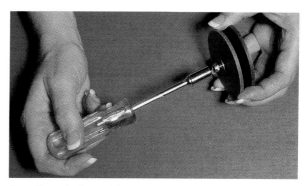

Installing a lock-nut joint.

"I've fallen down and I can't get up!" Use the largest joint the arms and legs will accommodate to avoid overly loose joints that won't support your bear while it is sitting.

Lock-nut Joints

① Cover the inside of the bolt with a matching sized disk and a metal washer.

② Finger-tighten a lock nut over this.

Lock nut joint.

~~~~ *Tip* ~~~~

Double-check the tightness of the lock-nut joints after the arms and legs have been stuffed. You may find that they feel much looser than they did prior to stuffing. Tighten them now if needed.

Make Your Own Epoxy Lock-nut Joints

Lock-nut joints will give you the most control over the tightness of the appendages on your bear. I also like them because they do not loosen over time. The drawback to this type of jointing system, however, is that the joints are difficult and awkward to install. But, by using epoxy glue, installation is made easy, and no special openings need to be left at the top of the legs and arms, or through the head, for the insertion of a screwdriver. Note: A quarter tube of glue will secure about twenty joints.

Fiberboard disks can be purchased from a teddy bear supply source. They come in many sizes and are pre-drilled with a hole in the center. You will need to purchase the correct size of screw to fit snugly into the center hole. I always use round-head screws that are 1 inch long.

① Purchase a double tube of quality five-minute epoxy. It pays to spend a few extra dollars here, because cheaper glues will not bond as well.

② Mix the glue per the manufacturer's instructions in a disposable, plastic mixing cup. Make sure your work area is well ventilated.

③ Insert the screw into the hole in the fiberboard disk. Apply a small amount of glue around the screw with a wooden craft stick and allow to dry.

④ Throw away your used mixing cups and wooden sticks.

To make large numbers of joints at one time, I punch holes, about 2 inches apart, through a 6-inch wide by 24-inch long strip of foamboard. I balance the ends of this strip on two paper cups and allow the screws to drop through these holes. I then set up all of the joints I am going to make before applying the epoxy. It is important to work quickly because the glue really does harden in five minutes!

Pop-rivet Joints

1 Insert a rivet through a metal washer, followed by a disk.

2 Inside the body, cover the rivet with a second disk, followed by another metal washer.

3 Using a pop-rivet tool, press the rivet until the excess snaps off.

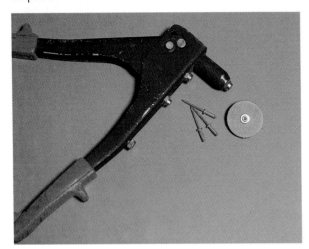

Use a pop-rivet tool for installing pop-rivet joints.

String Joints

This technique works well with smaller bears and when traditional joints are not available.

String jointing is a good alternative to safety or disk-type joints. It works especially well on small bears (14 inches tall and smaller).

1 Stuff all of the body parts to the desired firmness and sew them shut using a ladder stitch.

2 Use a long needle with a yard of heavy-duty thread, doubled and knotted at the end.

3 Begin on the left side of the body at the leg marking and secure the thread with a stitch and knot.

4 Sew through the body to the right side leg marking.

5 Sew through the right leg, exiting on the outer thigh. Return the needle into the same needle exit hole.

6 Sew through the leg and body and through the opposite leg at the joint marking. Repeat this process, sewing back and forth five to eight times.

7 Secure the thread with a stitch and a knot between the body and one of the legs so it cannot be seen. Bury the thread into the body. Repeat this process for the arms.

You can attach the head the same way by closing your running stitch tightly without the insertion of a joint into the neck opening, sewing any further openings around the neck shut with a whip stitch and manipulating your needle from the top of the head to a point between the legs.

For string joints, always try to use the same entrance and exit spots. The thread will be hidden from view on the outside of the bear, but it will catch on the stuffing inside, thereby holding the arms and legs on securely.

Button joints are a variation of a string joint. A button is simply added on the outside of each arm and leg during the jointing process for added interest.

For added interest and a "country" look, add buttons to the string joints on the outside of each arm and leg, like I did with this "country" angel.

Type of Joint	Special Tools Required	Difficulty of Installation	Tightness	Child-safe	Fine-tune
Cotter pin	Cotter key or needle nose plier.	Easy.	Moderate.	No.	Some.
Double cotter	Cotter key or needle nose pliers.	Easy.	Very wobbly.	No.	None.
Epoxy lock-nut	Ratchet.	Easy.	Loose to very tight.	No.	Yes.
Lock-nut	Ratchet and screwdriver.	Moderate to difficult.	Loose to very tight.	No.	Yes.
Plastic safety	None.	Easy.	Moderate.	Yes.	No.
Pop-rivet	Pop-rivet tool.	Moderate.	Moderate to very tight.	No.	No.
String	Long needle and thread.	Easy to moderate.	Loose to moderate.	Yes.	Some.
String and button	Long needle, thread, and buttons.	Moderate.	Loose to moderate.	No.	Some.

MARKING THE BEAR FOR ASSEMBLY

If your sewing has been less than perfect, double-check the joint markings for proper alignment. By doing this, you ensure that teddy's attached arms and legs will be the same length. To do this easily:

① Turn a leg inside out.

② Place the disk with the hole over the joint marking. The top of the disk should line up with the stitching at the top of the leg. If it doesn't, line up the top of the joint with the stitching. Make a new marking directly over the disk's hole on the teddy's leg. This will work for all types of joints, except for string.

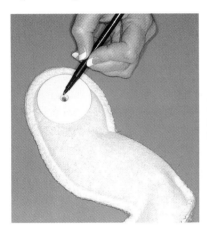

If necessary, make a new joint marking.

③ Repeat this process for the other leg and both arms. Also check the alignment of the markings inside the body.

④ Poke a hole through the markings, being careful to only pierce through one layer of fabric or fur.

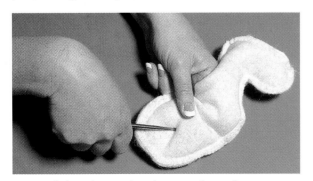

Pierce a hole with an awl or the point of very sharp scissors.

⑤ Insert the pegged portion of the joint, be it a screw, cotter pin, pop rivet, or safety peg, into the leg, so that the peg protrudes from the appendage to the fur or fabric's right side.

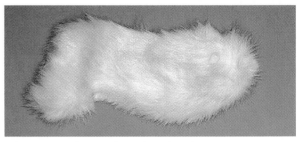

The peg should protrude to the right side.

⑥ Now place the peg into the body through the appropriate spot. Double-check the placement before attaching the locking devices.

⑦ Tighten the connections inside the body. Repeat this process for the remaining leg and arms.

Lock the washer attachment inside the body.

*W*hich way is forward?" Double-check the positioning of your bear's arms and legs before attaching the lock washers and other jointing mechanisms.

Installing the Neck Joint

1 Put a long piece of heavy-duty thread on your needle. Tie a knot in the two ends but leave a tail of about 6 inches, long enough for you to pull on later.

2 Sew a running stitch by hand, all the way around the base of the neck, leaving a 1/4-inch seam allowance. Each stitch should be about 1/4 inch long. When you get back to where you started, tie the two ends of the thread once, as if you were tying your shoelaces.

Sew a running stitch around the neck and insert the joint.

3 Insert the joint into the neck so the peg protrudes from the opening.

4 Pull both ends of the thread so the edge of the neck closes tightly around the peg. Secure the thread with several knots and trim. There should be no spaces around the peg large enough to insert your finger into. If you have a space, sew it shut using heavy-duty thread and a whip stitch. By closing this space well, you will be preventing your teddy's head from popping off in the future.

Pull the ends tight around the peg.

Keep the openings for the peg holes small and pull the running stitch very tightly around the peg to avoid a "pop-off" head!

5 Poke a hole through the top of the bear's body where the shoulder dart seams meet the front and back seams. You should have already left a small space here when you were sewing (from Chapter 4). Make sure your hole is in the top of the body, not the bottom, or you may have a very strange looking bear! To help you find the top, remember that the nap of the fur always runs down.

6 Insert the neck joint into the body.

7 On the inside of the body, cover the peg with another disk and closure according to the type of joint you are using. For safety joints, press the lock washer on as far as it will go. You should hear it click between two and four times. I find it helpful to put the bear's head upside down on a table and lean onto the joint until I hear it click.

8 Turn teddy's head so that it faces forward and smile back at it!

STUFFING

How firmly you stuff the bear's body is a matter of preference; there are no rules here. Regardless, place small amounts of stuffing at a time into the bear's arms, legs, and body. Use a stuffing stick to place small pieces of stuffing into tight spots such as toes, shoulders, and around joints. Try to keep the surface of your teddy smooth and lump-free as you go. Remember that stuffing is also the art of shaping your bear, so take your time.

Should you choose to use plastic pellets or glass beads, use a funnel, over a large bowl, to fill the parts. Don't over fill or you will lose some of that appealing "squishy" feeling. Plug each opening with a wad of fiberfill to keep the pellets in place while you sew the opening shut. Sew each part shut immediately after stuffing.

A traditional mohair bear stuffed with excelsior (wood wool) can take on a very appealing antique look and feel. If you are using it, stuff with small amounts, packing it down firmly as you go. A metal funnel can help keep the edges of your fabric from fraying during this process.

Use a bowl and funnel when stuffing a bear with pellets.

Tip

To repair a real fur pelt that has torn or split during the stuffing process, follow these steps:
* Glue the pelt down against the lining with tacky or leather glue.
* When dry, repair the tear with a small ladder stitch using a single strand of heavy-duty thread.
* Groom the surrounding fur with a stiff brush to cover the repair.

Tip

Stuff the feet and paws a little more firmly to help them retain shape through the years.

Stuffing is an exercise in shaping your bear; try not to overstuff it!

Closing the Seams

The final step!

1 Use heavy-duty thread, doubled on your needle, to close the seams.

2 Secure the thread at the bottom of the opening with a whip stitch.

3 Use a ladder stitch to close the seams.

4 Brush the seams (or use a long needle) to remove any fur trapped in the stitching.

Use a tool like this fingertip brush for grooming your bear. It is a small version of a wire dog grooming brush and can be purchased at teddy bear supply shops.

Tip

A small dog grooming brush works very well for grooming teddy bears! Gently brush the fur to remove fluff trapped in the stitching.

Congratulations!

The Projects

Page 59

Page 65

Page 77

Page 85

Page 93

Page 103

Page 113

Page 121

Page 121

Chapter 7

Projects

Up to this point, I have been describing the bear-making process to you. It is now time to tour the bear art gallery and select a design to make yourself. All of the finished bears are pictured here for you to view, and the patterns and any special instructions for each bear are included in this chapter.

The Beginner Bear is the easiest to make. I recommend choosing it if this is your first attempt at bear making. As I mentioned in Chapter 3, use a synthetic plush for a practice or trial-run bear; this will help you become familiar with the process and make you more confident when cutting into an heirloom fur coat later.

All of the bears can be easily made by anyone with some basic sewing skills. Even Truffles, who is a little more challenging, can be made by the novice bear maker with the patience to work carefully and the enthusiasm that is so very contagious among bear makers.

On a final note, bears, like people, can initially all look very much alike: they all have arms, legs, a head, and a body. Upon closer inspection, however, like a snowflake, no two are ever alike. A quarter-inch here, a nip or tuck there, and each bruin becomes an individual. Students in my classes are always surprised how a dozen or more people can all start with the same materials and pattern and end up creating uniquely different heirloom teddy bears.

Enjoy your bear-making experience as you sew life into this little creature!

The Beginner Bear is perfect for the first-time bear maker or the bear maker who wants to practice his or her skills before cutting into an heirloom fur coat. The sample was made from an inexpensive synthetic plush and stands about 14 inches tall.

Beginner Bear

Of all of the workshops I have taught, the most popular has been the Beginner Bear class. The Beginner Bear is an easy-to-make 14-inch tall design. It has no paw pads to sew and the pieces are wide enough to be turned easily. The teddy pictured here was made by my late father, who was 80 at the time! He made this bear from synthetic fur and used plastic safety eyes with an embroidered nose.

Follow the instructions in Chapters 3 through 6 to make your bear; there are also special instructions listed on the following page. Read through all instructions before beginning. Have fun!

Difficulty level: Very easy

You Will Need

1/4 yard of synthetic fur

Regular and heavy-duty thread

One set of eyes

One nose

Five sets of joints

Stuffing

Optional: Ribbon

Special Instructions

🐾 The Beginner Bear has no paw or foot pads; omit these steps (Chapter 4).

🐾 Sew the arms, right sides together, leaving an opening at the back as marked (Chapter 4).

🐾 Sew the legs, right sides together, all the way around, leaving only an opening at the back as marked. The bottom of the foot will be sewn shut (Chapter 4).

🐾 Tie a ribbon around your bear's neck.

Tip

If you are using safety eyes for this project, reinforce the fur fabric by placing a small scrap of cotton over the peg of each eye before snapping on the lock washers. This provides a little extra stability to the eyes and helps prevent them from wearing through the fabric over time.

VEST

You Will Need

1/8 yard of wool or washable felt

Several buttons

Marker

❶ Fold the wool or felt in half and place the vest pattern on the fold as marked. Pin the pattern in place and trace around it onto the felt.

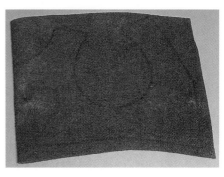

Trace the vest pattern onto the fabric.

❷ Cut out the vest.

❸ With right sides together, sew A to B on both sides. This will close the shoulder seams. Trim the seams to 1/8 inch. Turn the vest right side out and topstitch over the shoulder seams. Sew the buttons to the vest in a cluster.

Sew the shoulder seams.

Tip

A lady in one of my workshops sewed her son's old Boy Scout badges to the vest instead of buttons. She then presented the bear to him as a gift.

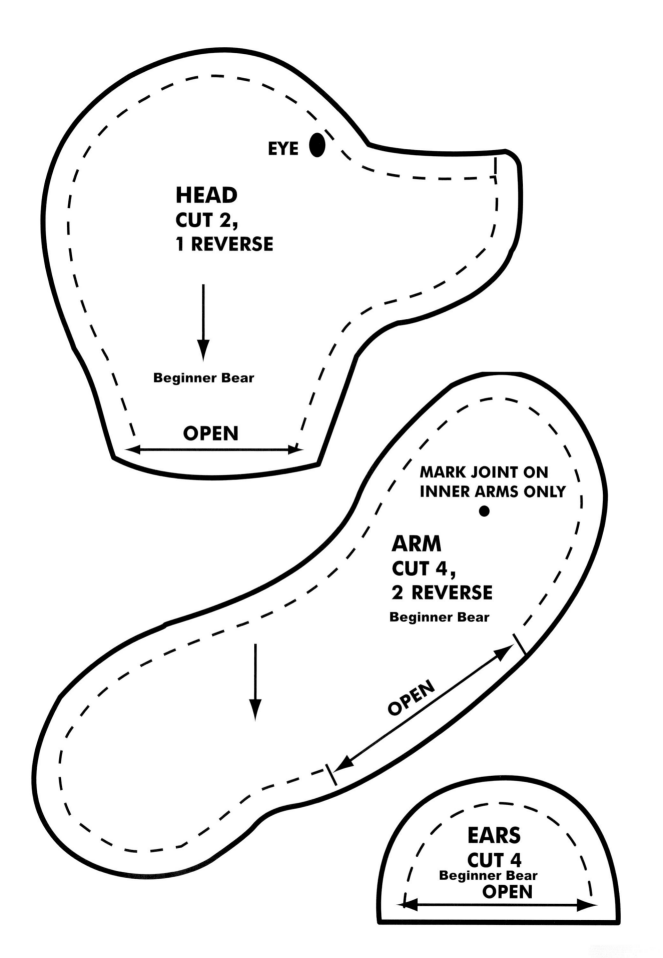

EYE ●

**HEAD
CUT 2,
1 REVERSE**

Beginner Bear

OPEN

**MARK JOINT ON
INNER ARMS ONLY**
●

**ARM
CUT 4,
2 REVERSE**

Beginner Bear

OPEN

**EARS
CUT 4**
Beginner Bear
OPEN

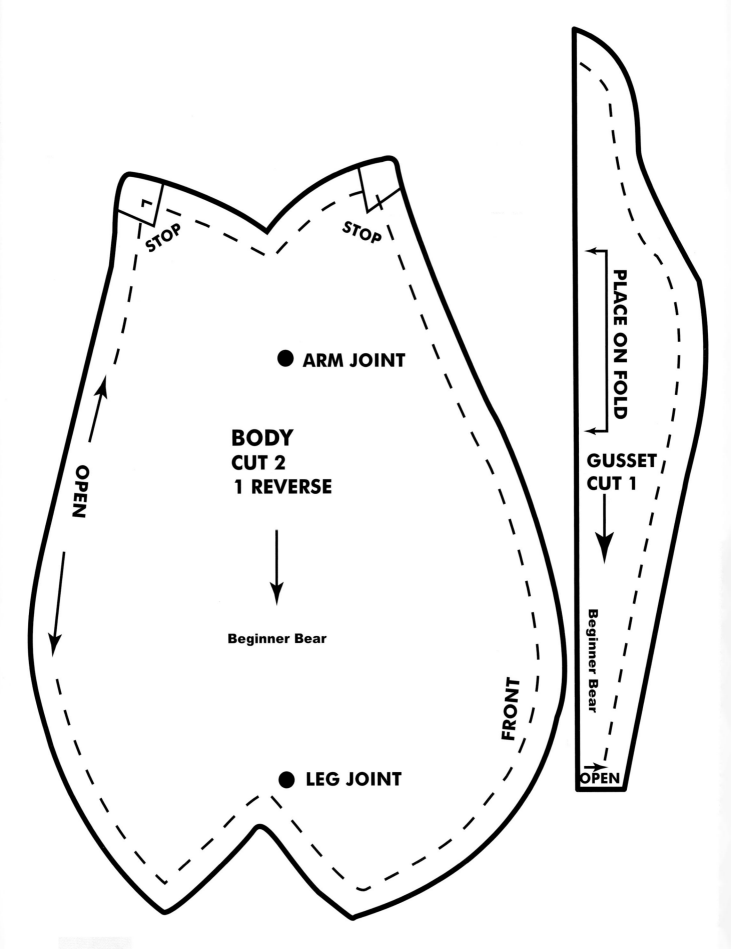

STOP

STOP

● ARM JOINT

BODY
CUT 2
1 REVERSE

Beginner Bear

OPEN

FRONT

● LEG JOINT

PLACE ON FOLD

GUSSET
CUT 1

Beginner Bear

OPEN

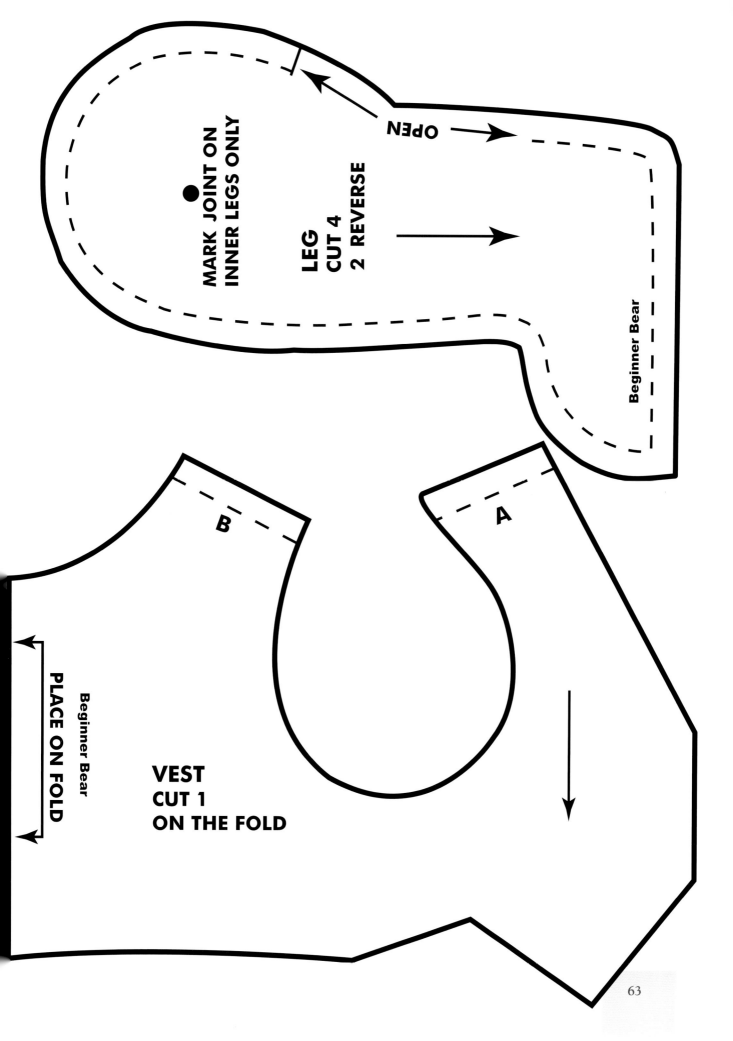

MARK JOINT ON
INNER LEGS ONLY

LEG
CUT 4
2 REVERSE

OPEN

Beginner Bear

B

A

Beginner Bear
PLACE ON FOLD

VEST
CUT 1
ON THE FOLD

63

Classic Ted, shown here in the library, with his long arms and legs, is modeled after bears made early in the twentieth century. I used an antique-looking gold mohair to make him. He has felt paw pads, an embroidered nose, and glass eyes. Ted is 30 inches tall; the pattern given makes a 15-inch version.

Project 2

Classic Ted

Early in the twentieth century, teddy bears were characterized by their long arms and legs and by the hump that so often defined their upper backs. With Classic Ted, I have tried to capture some of the look of yesteryear, while providing you with the versatility to modernize its appearance. This pattern has several options; for instance, you can shorten the muzzle if you like. Harry the Hiker and Gracie, shown on the following page, are both made from the shortened muzzle design. Enlarge or reduce this pattern as desired; it makes a 15-inch bear, but works well in all sizes. Gracie and Harry are 22 inches tall; the pattern was enlarged by 50 percent. Ted is 30 inches tall and made of mohair; the pattern was doubled. (See page 25 for information on altering pattern sizes.)

The overall proportions for this teddy are somewhat "human," which makes it easy to dress. I've used an old shirt collar and an ascot for Ted. By using the simple dress pattern provided, you can turn Ted into Gracie. You can also try on a pair of shoes; Harry the Hiker wears toddler's size 4 or 5. I made Harry's clothing from fleece scraps; have fun creating your own clothing for him. The possibilities of this bear are limited only by your imagination! Follow the instructions in Chapters 3 through 6 to make your bear.

Difficulty level: Easy

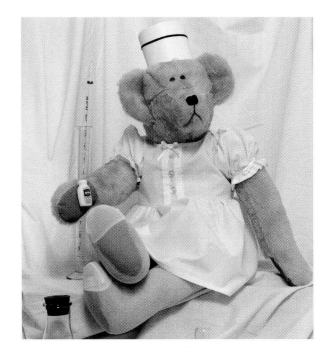

The Classic Nurse is 22 inches tall and made from inexpensive synthetic fur. Her dress is the same as Gracie's Simple Dress, but I omitted the slip, apron, and collar. I made her stockings out of white knee highs!

Gracie is made from luxurious dark brown mink. She has a "Take me home, please!" look... she's one of my favorites!

Here is Classic Ted made from mink. At 22 inches tall, this beautiful bear is adorned with a simple chiffon scarf.

Harry the Hiker is 22 inches tall and made from synthetic plush. I used the short muzzle pattern and safety eyes to make him. His shirt is made from scraps of polarfleece.

CLASSIC TED

You Will Need (for a 30-inch Bear)

3/4 yard of plush fabric or mohair or one hip-length fur coat
One set of eyes
One nose
Five sets of joints (2-inch disks)
12-inch square of fabric, leather, or felt for paw pads
Stuffing

Special Instructions

🐾 To make Classic Ted, use the pattern with the long muzzle. To make Gracie or Harry, use the pattern with the short muzzle.

🐾 If making Gracie, Harry, or a smaller bear, you will need less fabric.

TED'S COLLAR

You Will Need

Old white man's shirt
Scissors
Sewing machine

1 Cut the shirt collar just below the seam line, completely removing it. Reinforce the bottom edge of the collar by machine stitching very close to the edge. The size of the collar may need to be adjusted to fit your bear.

2 Cut the collar in half vertically and sew vertically across the back so the collar fits your bear. Trim the seam allowances and topstitch them down for a neater finish.

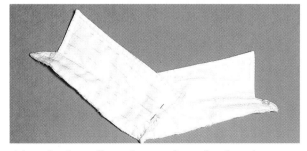

Adjust the shirt collar to fit around your bear's neck.

3 Button the collar around Ted's neck.

TED'S ASCOT

You Will Need

Scarf or rectangle of fabric cut to the desired length
Iron

1 Fold the edges of the scarf or fabric up 1/8 inch. Press.

2 Fold the edges up 1/4 inch and sew. The rectangle can be tapered in the center to prevent bunching under the collar.

3 Place the scarf around Ted's neck and secure it with a loose knot in the front.

GRACIE'S SIMPLE DRESS

This dress will fit a 20- to 22-inch teddy bear.

You Will Need

45-inch wide fabric:
    2/3 yard of patterned country print (overskirt)
    1/2 yard of contrasting country print (apron)
    2/3 yard of eyelet (slip)
Buttons, snaps, or Velcro
Small piece of iron-on interfacing
Ribbon trim
Sewing machine
Pins
Iron

Note: Use a 1/4-inch seam allowance unless otherwise stated.

1 Cut a rectangle of patterned country fabric 9 inches wide by 45 inches long for the overskirt.

2 Cut a rectangle of contrasting country fabric 8 inches wide by 12 inches long for the apron.

3 Cut a strip of contrasting fabric 6 inches high by 45 inches long for the apron tie.

4 Cut a rectangle of eyelet measuring 10 inches wide by 45 inches long for the slip.

5 Cut the bodice pattern from the patterned country fabric.

6 Cut the sleeves and collar from eyelet.

Note: Reinforce all sewing at the beginning and end with two or three backstitches.

7 With right sides together, sew the eyelet rectangle ends from the bottom to within 2 inches of the top.

8 Press these seams open. Topstitch around the 2-inch opening, 1/8 inch from the folded edge. Repeat Steps 7 and 8 for the overskirt.

For the back seam, topstitch the upper opening.

9 Fold the bottom edge of the eyelet slip under 1/8 inch. Press. Fold this edge under 1/4 inch and stitch in place to form a hem. Repeat for the overskirt.

Hem the skirt.

10 Sew two rows of the sewing machine's largest stitch around the top of the slip, leaving long threads at the start and finish. Do not reinforce the ends with a backstitch. Pull gently on both bobbin threads on one end. This will gather the upper edge of the slip. Repeat for the overskirt.

Gather the upper edge.

11 Iron two 1/2-inch wide strips of interfacing to the outer edges of the center back bodice pieces. Fold the edges under 1/2 inch and press. Pin the front and back bodice pieces, with right sides together. Sew the shoulder and side seams.

After ironing on the interfacing, sew the shoulder and side seams.

12 With right sides together, sew the collar pieces around the outside edge.

Sew the lower collar edges.

13 Turn the collar pieces right side out and press. Tack the two halves together at center top with a whip stitch. Center the collar over the right side of the bodice. Pin the collar in place. Fold the back facings over the right sides of the collar. Stitch through all thicknesses. Turn the facings right side out and press the seam allowance under. Topstitch along the upper edge.

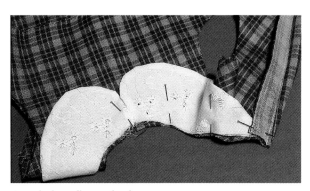

Attach the collar to the dress.

⓮ With right sides together, sew the sleeve ends. Make a hem along the bottom edge (see Step 10). Gather the upper edge of the sleeves. With right sides together, pin the sleeves to the

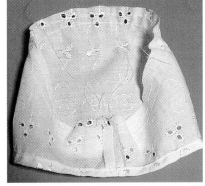

Sew the sleeve seam, hem the bottom, and gather the top edge.

arm holes, matching the side seams and the sleeve center with the shoulder seams. Adjust the fullness along the gathers and sew the sleeves in place.

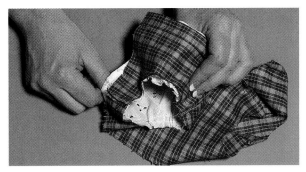

Sew in the sleeves.

⓯ Place the slip inside of the overskirt, matching the top gathered edges. Adjust the gathering so that both skirts measure the same length as the bottom of the bodice. Baste the two skirts together with both of the right sides facing up. With right sides together, pin the skirt ensemble to the bodice. Fold back the center back facings over the right side of the skirt. Stitch. Fold the facings right side out. Press the facings down and topstitch if desired. Close the back bodice using snaps, buttons, or Velcro closures. (If using snaps, you can cover the outer snaps with a button.)

Sew the skirt to the bodice.

⓰ Fold the long strip of contrasting fabric in half horizontally, with right sides together. Sew all around the open edges, leaving a 4-inch opening in the center.

⓱ Turn right side out and press. At the center opening, press the raw edges under 1/4 inch. This is the apron tie.

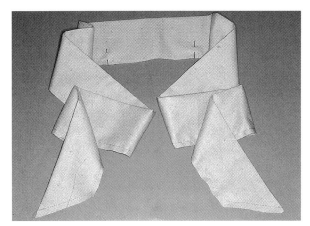

Make the apron ties.

⓲ Fold the side and bottom edges of the apron rectangle under 1/8 inch. Press. Fold these edges under 1/4 inch and stitch to form a hem. Gather the top of this piece so it measures 3-3/4 inches long. Insert the top of the apron into the tie opening. Baste in place. Machine stitch close to the open edge of the tie, catching the apron as you go.

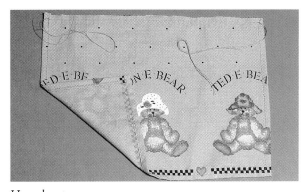

Hem the apron.

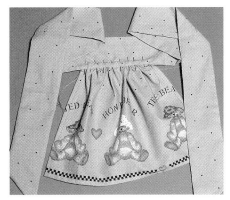

Sew the tie to the apron.

69

19 Finish the dress by sewing a small ribbon bow at the center of the collar. Tie matching ribbons around the sleeves and adjust their puffiness. Tie the apron over the skirts, using a big bow in the back.

Tip

This wedding dress was made with Gracie's Simple Dress pattern; I simply lengthened the skirt to touch the ground and omitted the apron. You can embellish the dress with lace and appliqués. My bear's dress is made from the satin of my own wedding dress and tulle from the veil. For this bear, I again used the short muzzle pattern. She is also 22 inches tall.

HAIR BOW

You Will Need

Two 4-inch squares of fabric
One 4-inch square of iron-on interfacing

1 Iron the interfacing to the wrong side of one of the squares to give the finished bow a little extra stability.

2 Sew the two squares together, leaving a 1/2-inch opening at center top.

3 Turn the square right side out through the small opening and press the seams.

4 Gather the center vertically. By hand, using a whip stitch, sew a small strip of fabric with its raw edges pressed under around the center of the bow. Stitch the bow to the bear's ear.

Making a hair bow is simple, yet it adds a special finishing touch to Gracie.

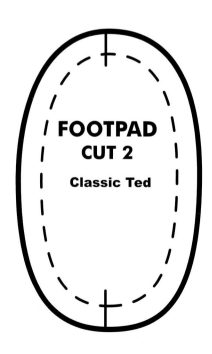

**FOOTPAD
CUT 2**

Classic Ted

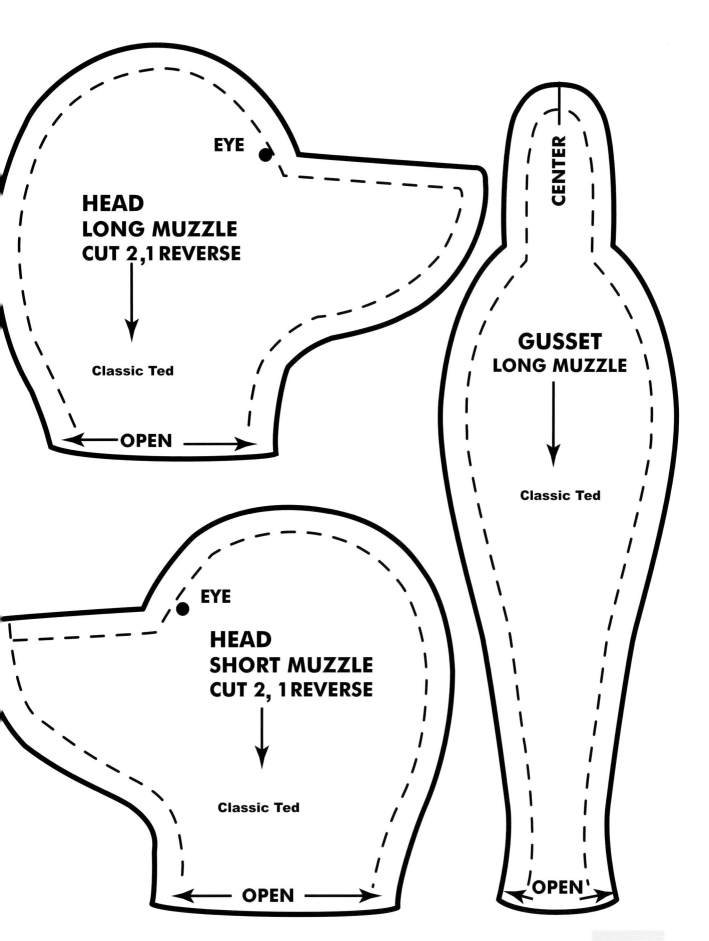

HEAD
LONG MUZZLE
CUT 2,1 REVERSE

EYE

Classic Ted

OPEN

GUSSET
LONG MUZZLE

CENTER

Classic Ted

OPEN

HEAD
SHORT MUZZLE
CUT 2, 1 REVERSE

EYE

Classic Ted

OPEN

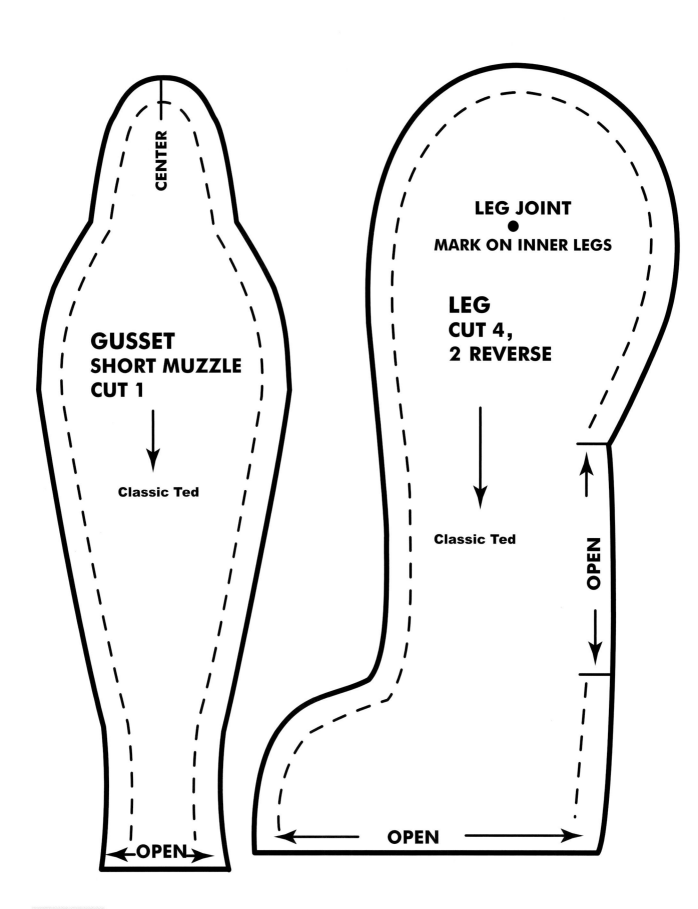

CENTER

GUSSET
SHORT MUZZLE
CUT 1

Classic Ted

OPEN

LEG JOINT
●
MARK ON INNER LEGS

LEG
CUT 4,
2 REVERSE

Classic Ted

OPEN

OPEN

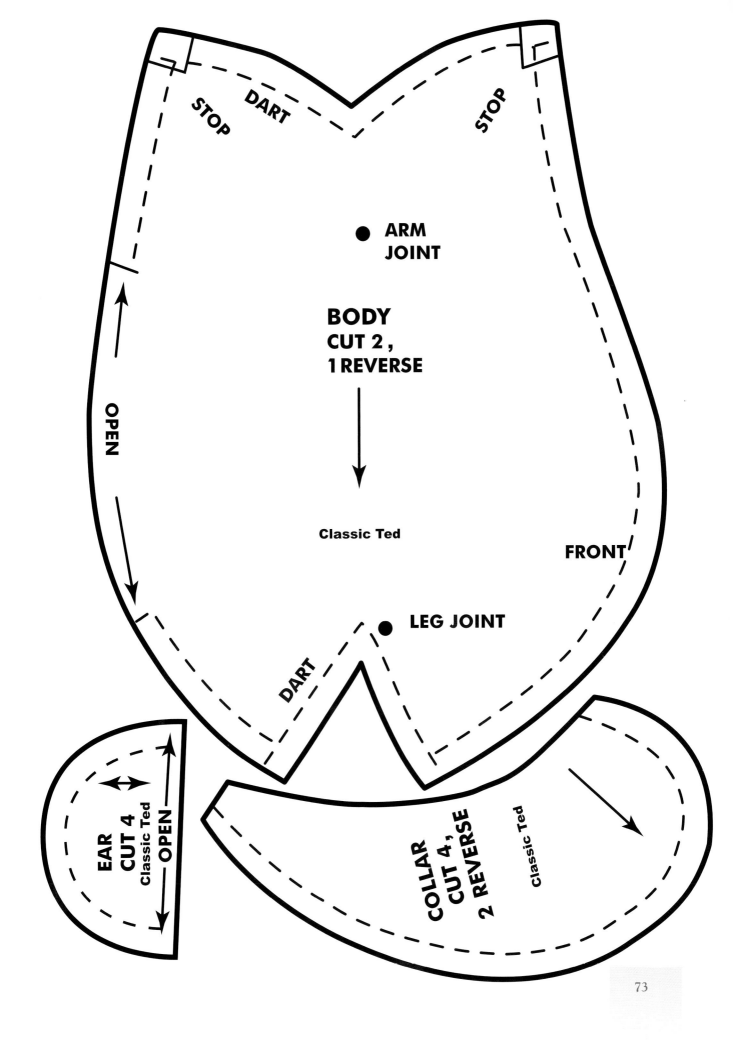

STOP

DART

STOP

● ARM
JOINT

BODY
CUT 2 ,
1 REVERSE

OPEN

Classic Ted

FRONT

● LEG JOINT

DART

EAR
CUT 4
Classic Ted
OPEN

COLLAR
CUT 4,
2 REVERSE

Classic Ted

73

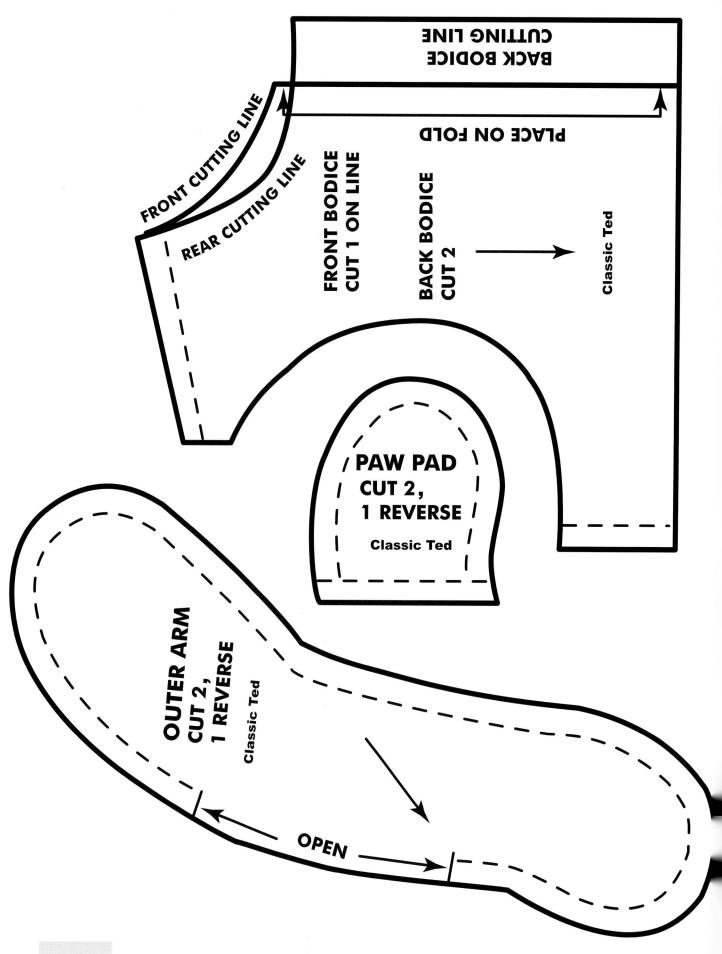

BACK BODICE
CUTTING LINE

FRONT CUTTING LINE

REAR CUTTING LINE

PLACE ON FOLD

FRONT BODICE
CUT 1 ON LINE

BACK BODICE
CUT 2

Classic Ted

PAW PAD
CUT 2,
1 REVERSE

Classic Ted

OUTER ARM
CUT 2,
1 REVERSE

Classic Ted

OPEN

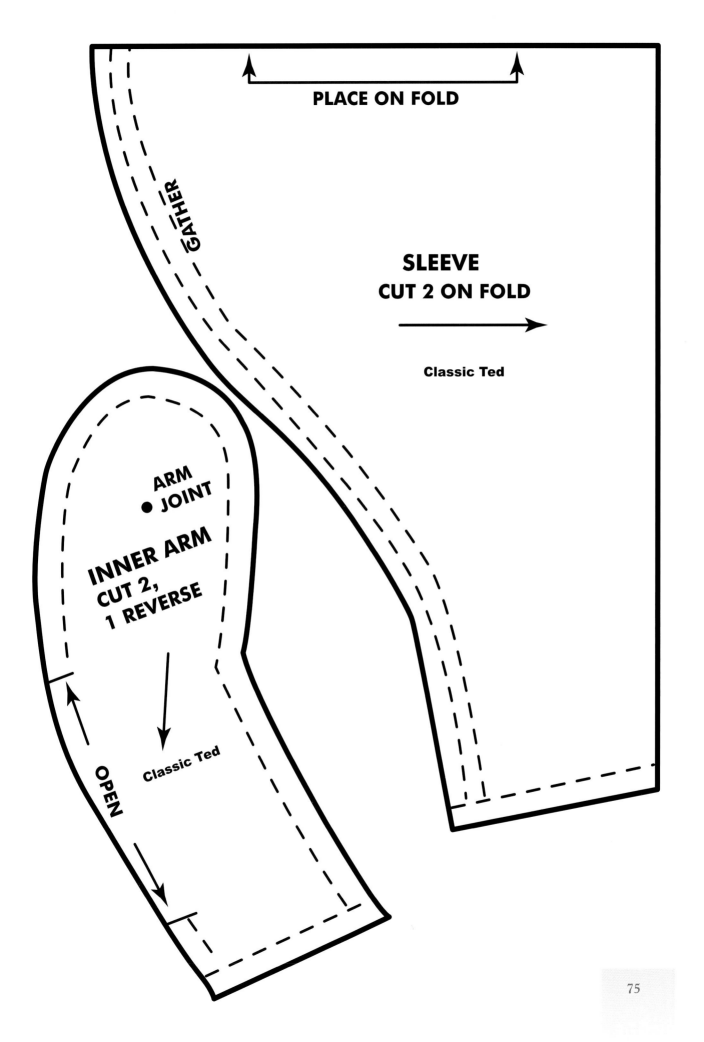

PLACE ON FOLD

GATHER

SLEEVE
CUT 2 ON FOLD

Classic Ted

ARM
● JOINT

INNER ARM
CUT 2,
1 REVERSE

Classic Ted

OPEN

The 14-inch pandas pictured here were made with a beautiful black mink coat and a white knee-length mink paw coat. From the two coats, six panda bears were made!

Project 3

Panda-Mania

The panda bear is a wonderful way to stretch the use of your fabrics; you can use fur collars and hats that would otherwise be too small to make an entire bear alone, because each part requires only a small amount of fur.

Any teddy pattern can be made into a panda bear by simply using the eye patch and two colors of fur. The arms, legs, ears, and eye patches are made from the darker, or contrasting, color of fabric. The bear does not have to be black and white; use your imagination with the colors. A pink and white or blue and white teddy would make an adorable baby gift. Try black and red for a modern look; dress it in a red or black plaid vest made from the pattern on page 60, and wow—instant charisma!

Follow the instructions in Chapters 3 through 6 to make your bear; there are also special instructions for this bear listed on the following page.

Difficulty level: Easy

This little clown bear is made from red and white mink coats.

PANDA-MANIA

Special Instructions

🐾 Cut the head, gusset, and body pieces from the white fur. Cut the eye, ear, arm, and leg pieces from the black fur.

🐾 When sewing the paw pads onto the bear, use a color of thread that matches the pad material.

🐾 Sew the panda's head per the instructions in Chapter 4.

Sewing the Legs

❶ Fold the leg in half along the fold line.

❷ Stitch from the tip of the toe to the top (at the back of the leg), as shown on the pattern.

❸ Leave an opening at the *front* of the leg (as shown on the pattern) for inserting the joint and stuffing later.

❹ Tack the paw pad to the leg at the center front seam and at the center back (on the fold line). Sew the pad into the opening by hand using heavy-duty thread and a backstitch.

Sewing the Arms

❶ Sew the paw pad to the short inner arm side of the pattern piece. Once sewn, the inner arm should "mirror" the connected outer arm.

❷ Fold the arm in half along the fold line.

❸ Stitch the arm shut along the stitch lines shown on the pattern.

❹ Leave an opening at the *front* of the arm (as shown on the pattern) for inserting the joint and stuffing later.

Although the openings in the arms and legs for the Panda are at the front of the pattern pieces, it is assembled just like the other bears in this chapter. Be sure to close the openings neatly, because they are in more visible positions.

🐾 The eye patches must be attached before the eyes are inserted:

Installing the Panda's Eyes

❶ Begin by piercing a small hole over the eye marking on the patch using an awl. Trim the fur to 1/8 inch around this hole. (The spots of fur you will trim are about the size of a pencil eraser.)

Surprise! Check the positioning of the patches before installing them to avoid this surprised teddy look!

Pierce holes in the eye patches.   *Trim the fur.*

❷ For plastic safety eyes, from the right side, insert the peg though the mark in the patch, and then through the head, before stuffing it. Be sure that the inner curve of the patch faces toward the nose before snapping on the lock washers.

❸ For glass eyes, stuff the head first. Insert the needle into the head behind the ear and exit at the opposite eye. Place the needle in the wrong side of the hole in the eye patch and pick up the glass eye's loop on the right side. Squeeze the loop gently shut with pliers. Direct your needle back through the hole in the eye patch, through the eye marking on the head, and back up toward the opposite ear. Maneuver the eye through the holes in both the patch and the head. A dab of glue on the head's eye marking will help secure the eye. Finish the glass eyes per the instructions in Chapter 5.

❹ Trim a section of fur 1/2 inch wide and 1 inch long, straight down from each eye. Put a bit of tacky glue on these sections and secure the patches to them.

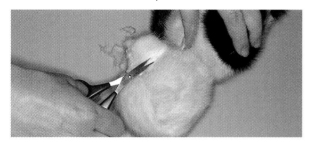

Trim the fur.

❺ Thread a 4-inch needle with doubled heavy-duty thread, knotted at the end.

❻ Beginning under one of the eye patches, sew back and forth across the head and through the eye patches to further hold them into place. Begin near the bottom of the patch and work your way up. Try to leave only very small stitches on the right sides of the patch because these can be easily hidden in the fur.

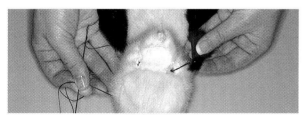

Insert the needle through the head, then the eye patch, and then the glass eye loop.

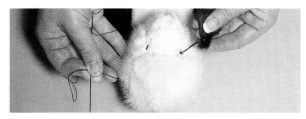

Sew back through the patch and head, ending near where the ear will be.

❼ Knot off your final stitch and bury the thread in the bear's head.

❽ Brush and groom the eye area with a stiff brush.

🐾 Finish the panda by putting 1-1/4 yards of beautiful ribbon or lace trim with a small silk flower around its neck.

This panda is made from synthetic fur, using the pattern for Auntie Bear-nadette (page 85).

I made this sample from mohair.

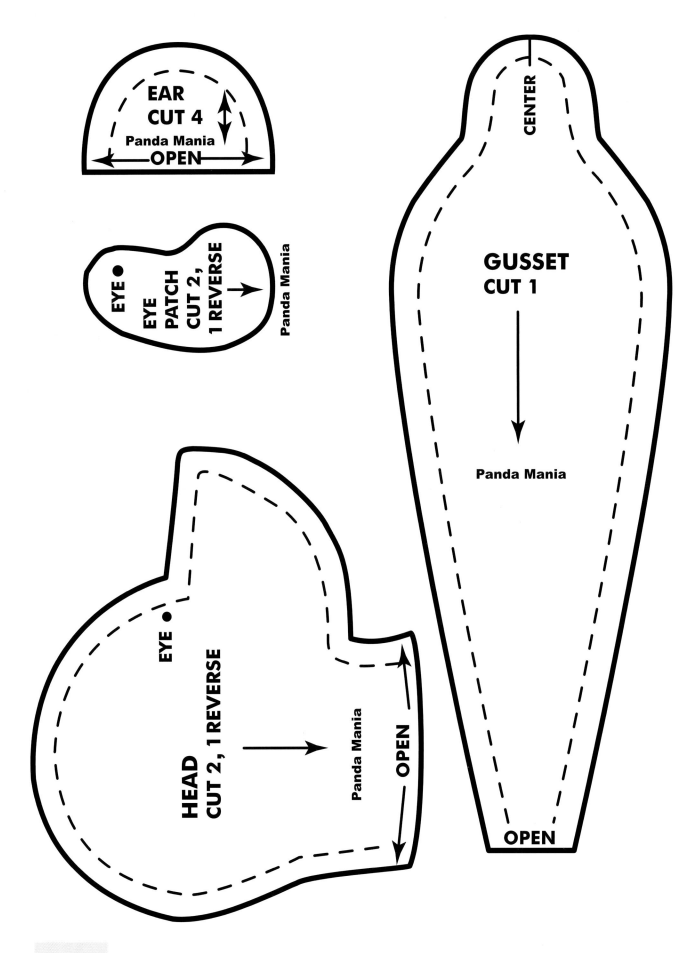

EAR
CUT 4
Panda Mania
OPEN

EYE ●
EYE
PATCH
CUT 2,
1 REVERSE
Panda Mania

GUSSET
CUT 1
Panda Mania
CENTER
OPEN

EYE ●
HEAD
CUT 2, 1 REVERSE
Panda Mania
OPEN

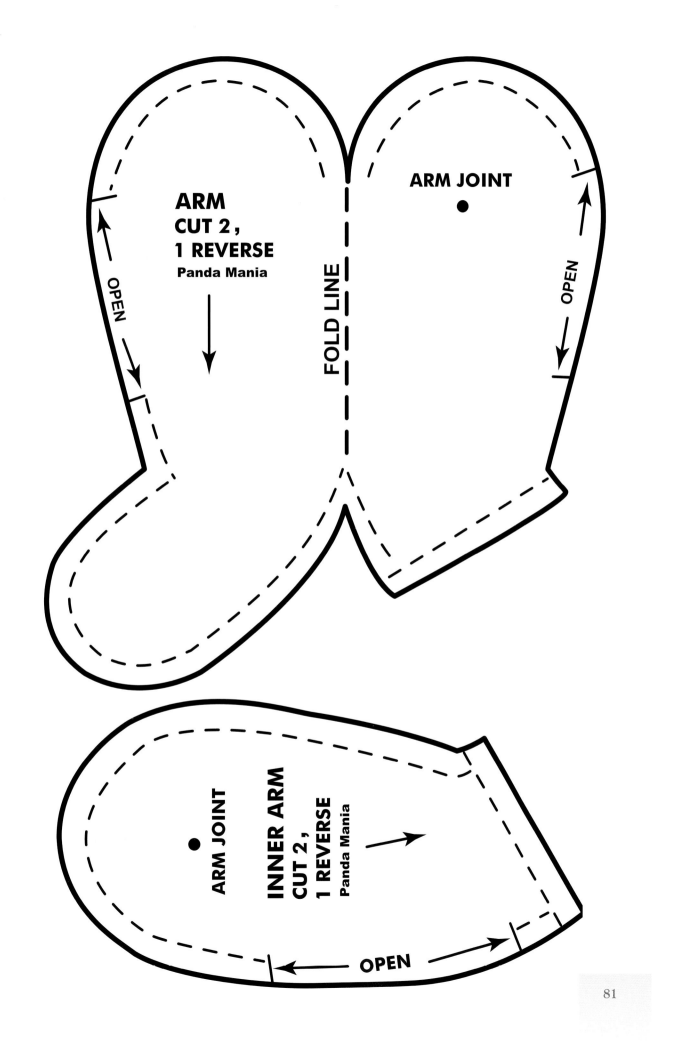

ARM
CUT 2 ,
1 REVERSE
Panda Mania

OPEN

ARM JOINT

OPEN

FOLD LINE

OPEN

ARM JOINT

INNER ARM
CUT 2 ,
1 REVERSE
Panda Mania

OPEN

81

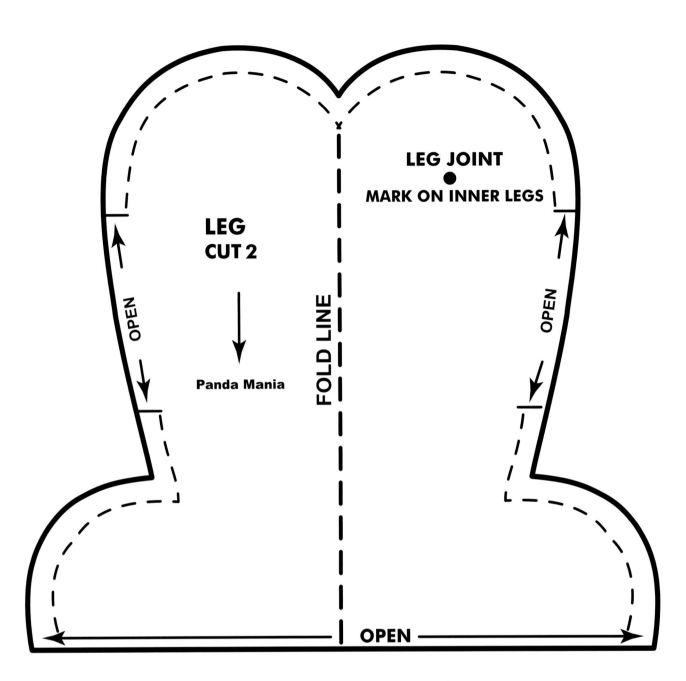

LEG
CUT 2

LEG JOINT
MARK ON INNER LEGS

OPEN

OPEN

FOLD LINE

Panda Mania

OPEN

PAW PAD
CUT 2,
1 REVERSE
Panda Mania

FOOTPAD
CUT 2
Panda Mania

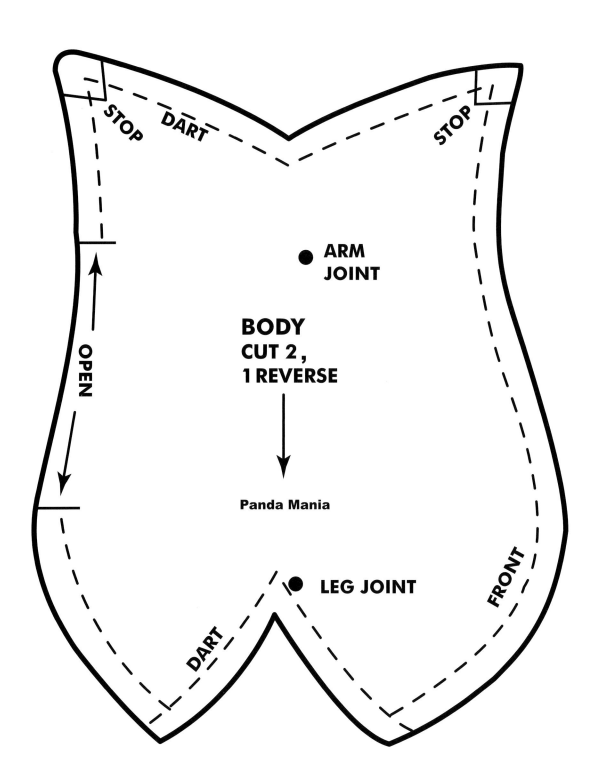

STOP

DART

STOP

ARM JOINT

BODY
CUT 2,
1 REVERSE

OPEN

Panda Mania

LEG JOINT

DART

FRONT

Auntie Bear-nadette is ready for afternoon tea! She is 17 inches tall and made from a mink jacket. I found her stole in an antique store; it fits her perfectly. She wears purchased spectacles over her glass eyes. The nose is embroidered.

Project 4

Auntie Bear-nadette

Once a year I travel to Southern Ontario to visit my sister. It has become a tradition to spend an afternoon or two trekking to all of the wonderful antique shops, boutiques, and tea rooms in her area. On one such trip, I came across a fur stole made with six tiny animals, all of which still had their heads and tails. Holding the stole, I felt certain that at some time in the past, this must have been a treasured bit of finery in one elegant woman's fur collection. I blew the dust from the price tag, paid the shopkeeper, and took the fur home with me, unsure of what I was going to do with it.

The stole hung in my workshop for well over a year. Then, in the dead of winter, Auntie Bear-nadette was born. She was 17 inches tall and rather matronly looking with her red mink fur, veiled hat, and spectacles, but she needed a special finishing touch. I eyed one of the tiny animals on the stole, removed it from the group, and clipped it around the bear's neck. Instantly, she had achieved a perfectly polished Victorian look, and my antique stole had found a valuable new purpose as a part of this treasured bear-loom.

Follow the instructions in Chapters 3 through 6 to make your bear.

Difficulty level: Easy

AUNTIE BEAR-NADETTE

You Will Need

Mink jacket or stole or 1/3 yard of plush fur or mohair
One set of eyes
One nose
Five sets of joints
Fabric or leather of your choice for paw pads
Stuffing
Pelt stole or fur collar
Heavy-duty thread
Optional: Purchased spectacles

Special Instructions

🐾 Put a pair of spectacles on the bear.

🐾 You can make a shawl for your bear by draping a boa from a stole on its shoulders. Many boas will still have the clips attached below the head, allowing you to fasten the head to the tail. One or two stitches with heavy-duty thread will also secure the stole. You can also fasten a fur collar around the bear's neck with a piece of old jewelry.

AUNTIE BEAR-NADETTE'S HAT

You Will Need

Fun foam*
8- by 6-inch piece of hat netting
Ribbon, feathers, and flowers
Low-temperature glue gun or thick tacky glue

*Fun foam is available at any craft supply store. It is a pliable, soft foam that makes the perfect hat!

❶ Cut a strip of fun foam 12 inches long by 1-1/2 inches wide. Overlap the two ends 1 inch and glue in place.

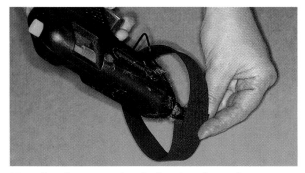

Use a hot glue gun to glue the foam's ends together.

❷ Gather the hat netting along one of the 8 inch sides. Glue this over the fun foam's seam.

❸ Glue a piece of ribbon trim over the fun foam, so the ends meet at the hat netting.

You can embellish the hat with ribbons, flowers, or whatever you wish!

❹ You can decorate the front of the hat by adding silk flowers and feathers over and under the netting. Arrange the netting so it falls gently over the flowers.

❺ Perch the hat on the bear.

I made this muskrat teddy from the Panda-Mania pattern, except I omitted the eye patches. She wears a fox collar. Notice the coat owner's initials on the paw.

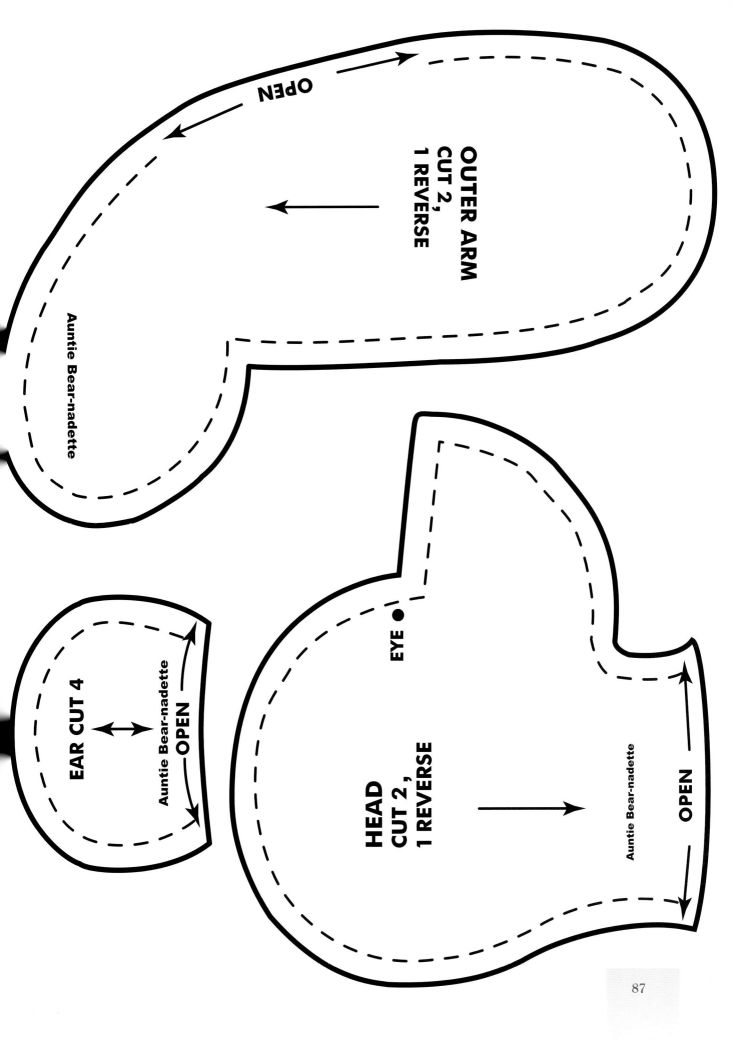

OUTER ARM
CUT 2,
1 REVERSE

OPEN

Auntie Bear-nadette

EAR CUT 4

Auntie Bear-nadette
OPEN

HEAD
CUT 2,
1 REVERSE

EYE ●

Auntie Bear-nadette

OPEN

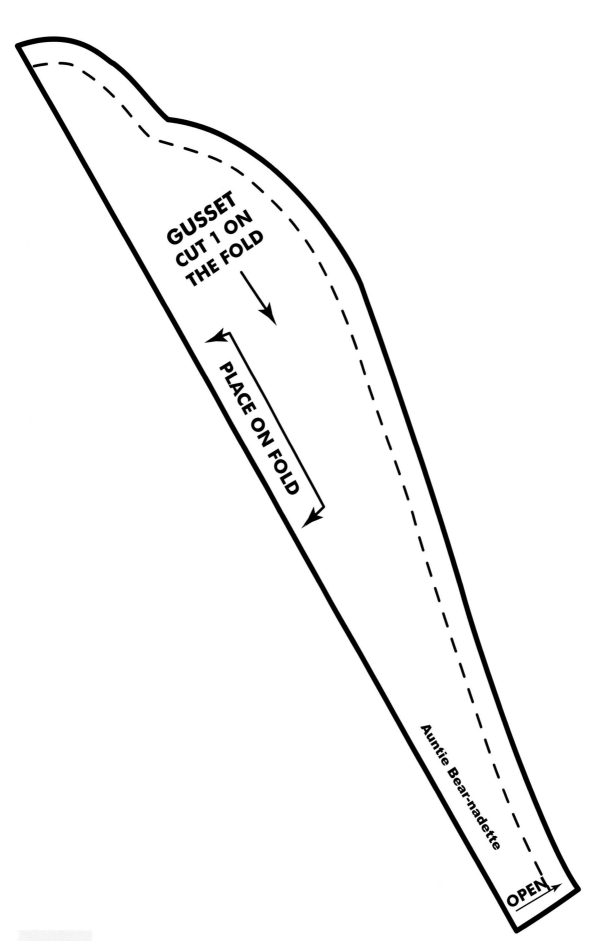

GUSSET
CUT 1 ON
THE FOLD

PLACE ON FOLD

Auntie Bear-nadette

OPEN

88

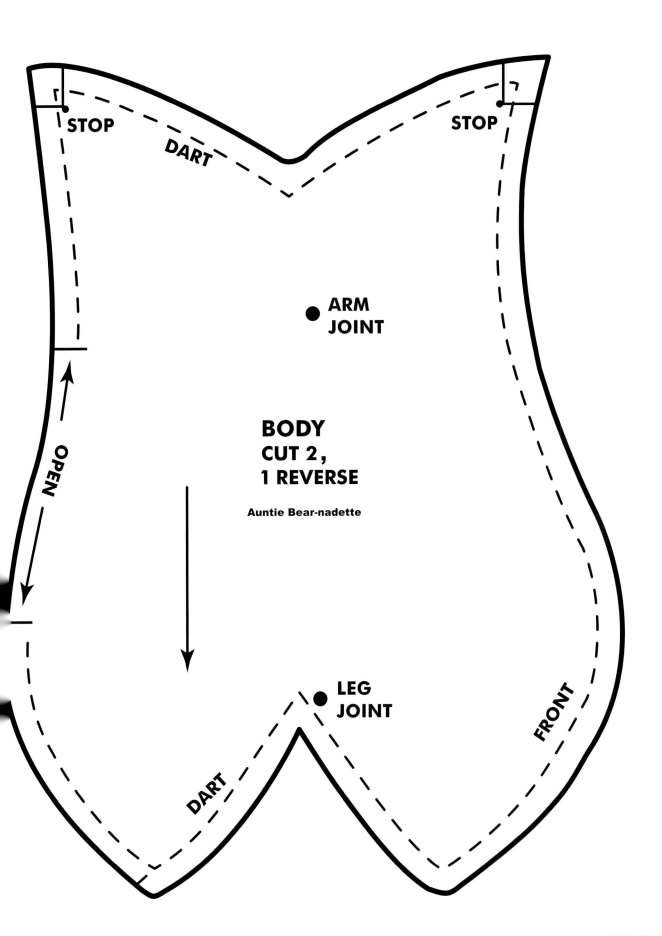

STOP

STOP

DART

ARM
JOINT

OPEN

BODY
CUT 2,
1 REVERSE

Auntie Bear-nadette

LEG
JOINT

DART

FRONT

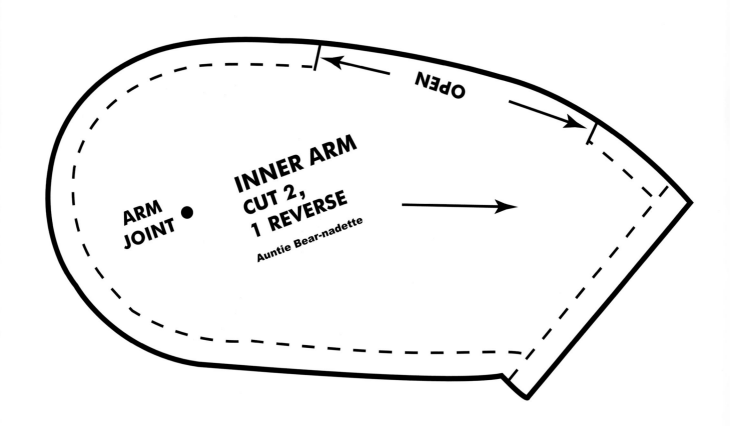

INNER ARM
CUT 2,
1 REVERSE
Auntie Bear-nadette

ARM
JOINT ●

OPEN

PAW PAD
CUT 2,
1 REVERSE

Auntie Bear-nadette

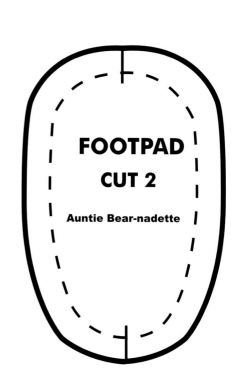

FOOTPAD
CUT 2

Auntie Bear-nadette

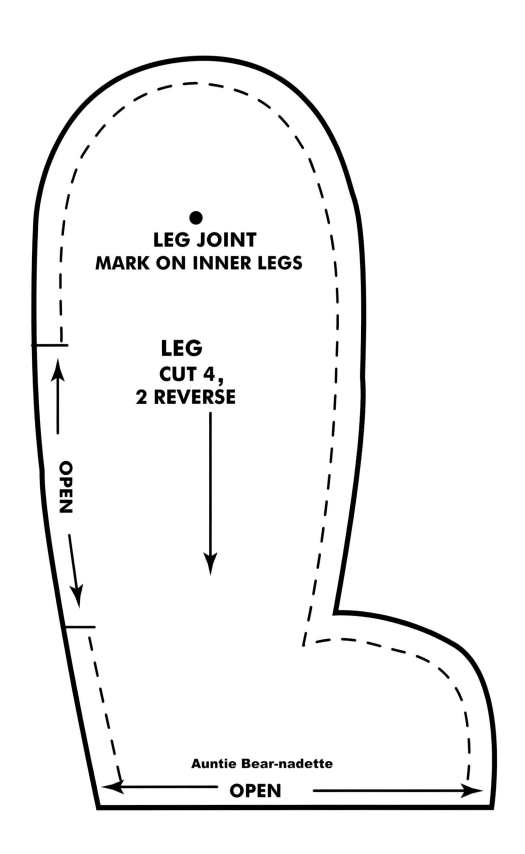

LEG JOINT
MARK ON INNER LEGS

LEG
CUT 4,
2 REVERSE

OPEN

Auntie Bear-nadette

OPEN

Charlotte O'Bear is a stylized, modern-looking bear. I used a white mink stole to make her. She has a large-brimmed hat trimmed in silk flowers. I inserted a music box into her body for an added charming element.

Project 5

Charlotte O'Bear

*S*ome of my favorite trinkets from days gone by include a pair of lace gloves, an old beaded purse, and my mother's faux pearl necklace. All are carefully kept in an equally aged pine chest. Another one of my favorite things, Charlotte O'Bear, sits atop an antique quilt, purchased at a flea market, near the chest.

This very feminine, stylized teddy bear is 17 inches tall, fully jointed like the other bears, and wears a large wire-brimmed hat trimmed with flowers. She is shown here made from a white mink stole. The pattern for Charlotte works especially well in mink and mohair. Despite her modern design, she retains an air of nostalgia. I've stuffed her with polyester fiberfill and scented plastic pellets, adding to her boudoir charm. Finally, her hat keeps her in full Victorian ladylike style; I used taffeta and lace, but you can choose velveteen or any other luxury fabric with a bit of body.

Charlotte O'Bear also has a secret! Wind up her little tail and a hidden music box plays a favorite tune. In this case, it's "My Favorite Things," of course!

Follow the instructions in Chapters 3 through 6 to make your bear; there are also special instructions for this bear listed below.

Difficulty level: Intermediate

I used pink mohair for this version of Charlotte O'Bear; I call her Charmaine.

93

CHARLOTTE O'BEAR

You Will Need

1/3 yard of plush fabric or mohair, a small fur coat, or waist-length stole

One pair of eyes

One nose

8-inch square of fabric of your choice for paws

Stuffing

1-inch square of cotton muslin

Optional: Plastic pellets

One music box with a 1-inch or longer key

One grommet and installation tool (purchase these at a fabric store)

Hammer

Special Instructions

🐾 Stuff one of the arms at the paw and shoulder with polyester fiberfill. Loosely fill the center area of the arm with pellets, using a funnel over a large bowl. Place a small bit of fiberfill over the pellets and sew the arm shut using a ladder stitch. Repeat this process with the other arm and both legs, sewing each part closed as you stuff it. Use only fiberfill in the body because pellets may interfere with the music box.

🐾 The following are directions for inserting the music box:

❶ Leave a small space at the music box marking when sewing the body, as shown on the pattern. Place a 1-inch square of cotton muslin behind this hole and pierce a hole through it.

❷ Insert the top portion of the grommet through both the muslin and fur from the right side and snap on the grommet back portion inside the body. Using the installation tool, and several taps with a hammer, secure the grommet in place.

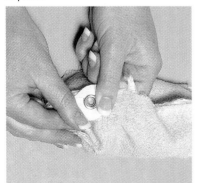

Use a grommet to insert the back.

A few taps of the hammer should set the grommet securely into place.

❸ If you do not have a grommet, you can sew all around the opening using a whip stitch. Place them very close together so the end result resembles a button hole. This prevents fur from becoming trapped in the key mechanism as it turns.

❹ With right sides together, sew around the edge of the tail, leaving the straight edge open.

❺ Turn the tail right side out and insert the key into it. Whip stitch the straight edge shut, folding under the raw edges as you sew.

❻ Secure the triangle of the key into an upright position by sewing it into place inside the tail. To do this, sew through both layers of the tail, around the top portion of the key. The fur will hide your stitches as long as you keep them small.

❼ Place the key through the grommet into the body. Turn the key into the appropriate opening of the music box until you hear the music play. The steps are pictured here without the tail attached to the key to allow the detail to be more clearly seen.

The key should fit inside the tail.

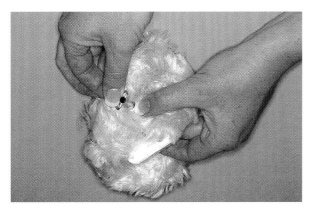

Wind the key to the music box.

❽ Continue to assemble the bear as shown in Chapter 6. Surround the music box with polyester fiberfill while stuffing.

CHARLOTTE'S HAT

You Will Need

Silk flowers, leaves, lace, pearl strands
1/4 yard of fabric
1- by 14-inch piece of bristol board
1 yard of organza ribbon
24-gauge crafter's wire
Marker
Scissors
Tacky glue
Safety glasses

❶ Transfer the patterns onto the fabric and cut out the pieces.

❷ With the right sides together, sew the back edges of both of the brim sections. Match these seams and, with right sides together, sew the two brim sections around the outer edge.

❸ Cut a long piece of 24-gauge crafter's wire. Whip stitch the wire onto the outer seam allowance. You can also secure the wire by machine, using a large zigzag stitch. Wear safety glasses and go slowly so you don't break your needle by striking the wire.

❹ Once you have sewn all around the edge, smooth the wire circle between your fingers. Twist the two ends together and cut off any excess wire. Fold the ends down and secure them in place with a few more stitches.

❺ Turn the brim right side out and press the sewn edge. Topstitch the outer edge 1/4 inch from the seam.

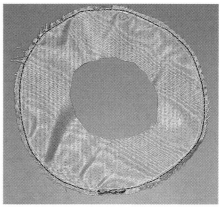

The outer brim seam with the wire attachment.

The brim is now turned and topstitched.

❻ Sew the ends of the hat band, right sides together.

The hat band's back seam.

7 Using a running stitch, gather the outer edge of the hat top. With right sides together, sew the top to the upper edge of the hat band easing any fullness as you sew. Trim the seam allowances.

The hat top and band are now sewn together.

8 Pin the right side of the brim to the right side of the hat band. Stitch the two together by machine or by hand using a backstitch. Turn the seam allowance up toward the hat band and topstitch on the band.

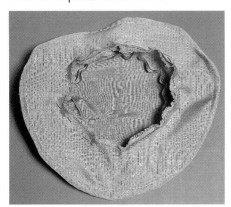

Here, the band is sewn to the brim.

9 Curve the bristol board into place inside the hat band and keep it securely in place with a dab of tacky glue. Trim off any excess board with the scissors.

10 Sew two lengths of organza ribbon to the hat band's side seam allowances. Trim the hat by gluing on flowers, leaves, lace, and pearl strands. Finish the hat by smoothing the wire circle with your fingers. Tie it on the bear using a large bow. Trim any excess organza.

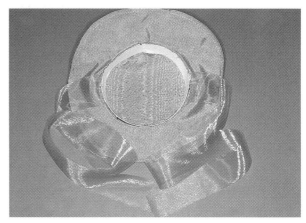

Attach ribbons to the inside of the hat.

Ribbon ties are attached to the hat. Floral decorations are glued on for the finishing touch.

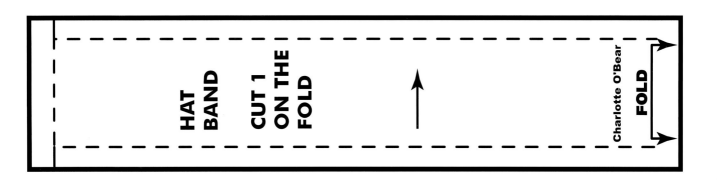

HAT BAND
CUT 1 ON THE FOLD

Charlotte O'Bear
FOLD

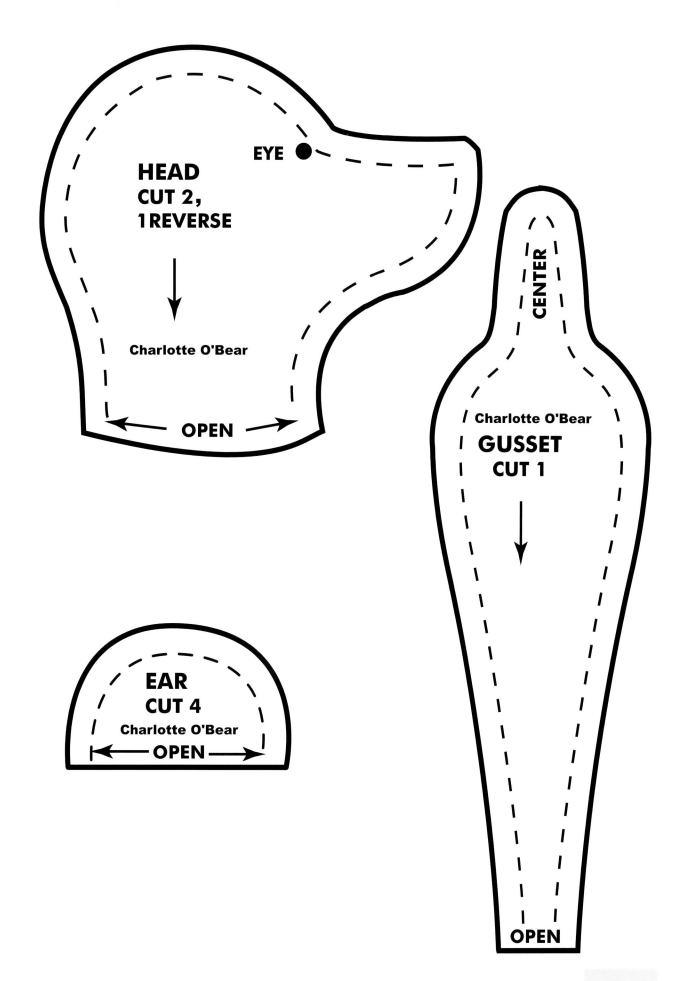

HEAD
CUT 2,
1REVERSE

EYE ●

Charlotte O'Bear

← **OPEN** →

CENTER

Charlotte O'Bear
GUSSET
CUT 1

EAR
CUT 4
Charlotte O'Bear
← **OPEN** →

OPEN

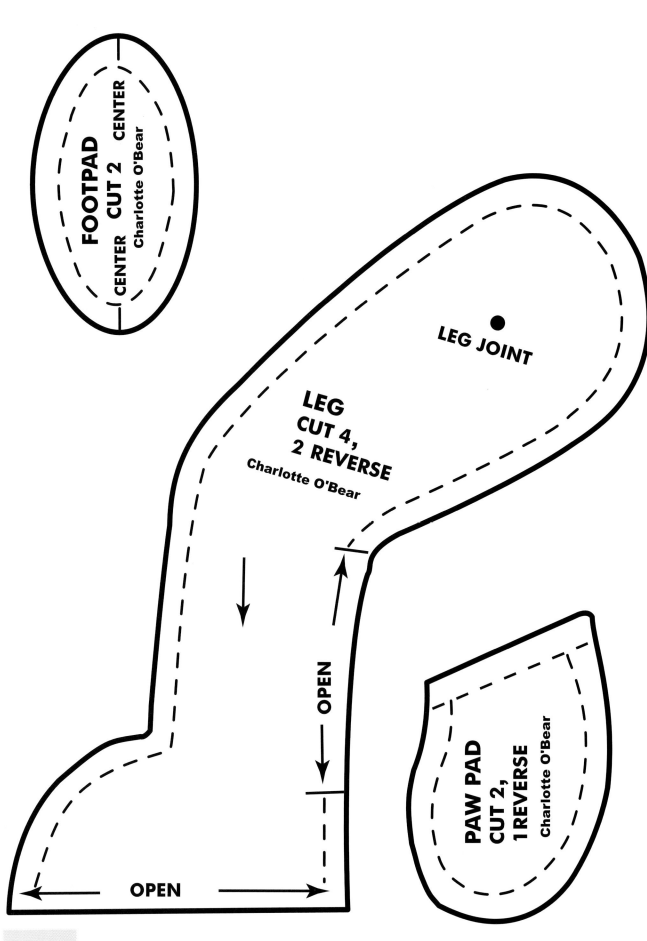

FOOTPAD CUT 2
CENTER   CENTER
Charlotte O'Bear

LEG
CUT 4,
2 REVERSE
Charlotte O'Bear

LEG JOINT

OPEN

OPEN

PAW PAD
CUT 2,
1 REVERSE
Charlotte O'Bear

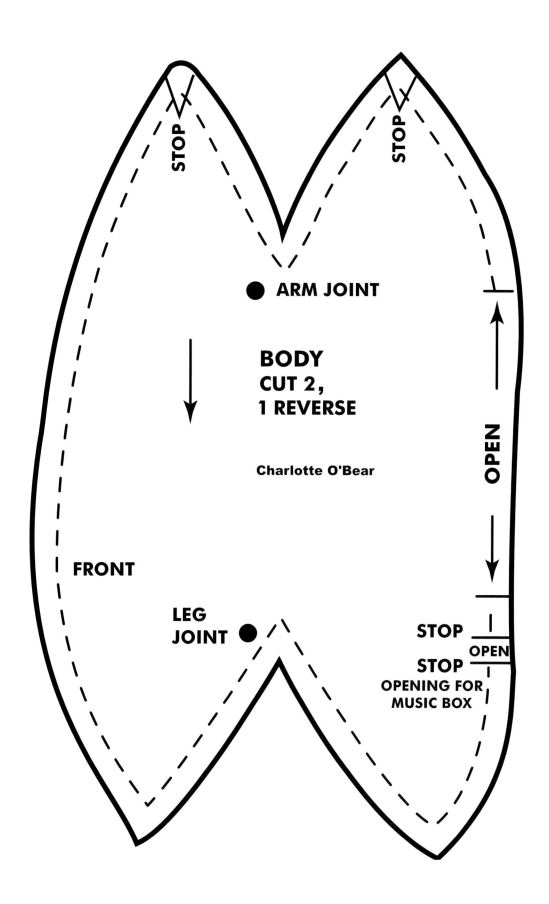

STOP

STOP

● ARM JOINT

BODY
CUT 2,
1 REVERSE

Charlotte O'Bear

OPEN

FRONT

LEG
JOINT ●

STOP

OPEN

STOP

OPENING FOR
MUSIC BOX

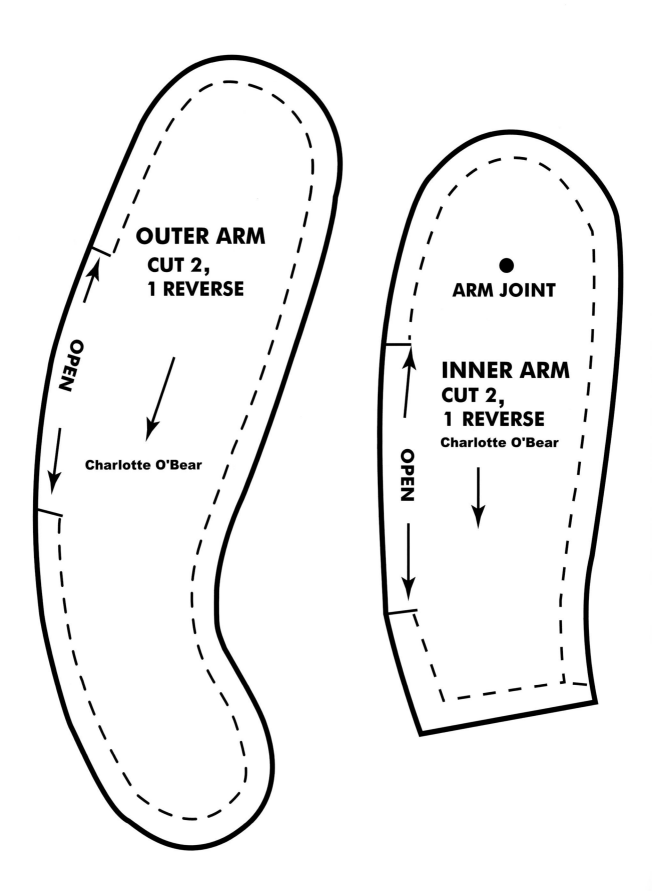

OUTER ARM
CUT 2,
1 REVERSE

OPEN

Charlotte O'Bear

ARM JOINT

INNER ARM
CUT 2,
1 REVERSE

Charlotte O'Bear

OPEN

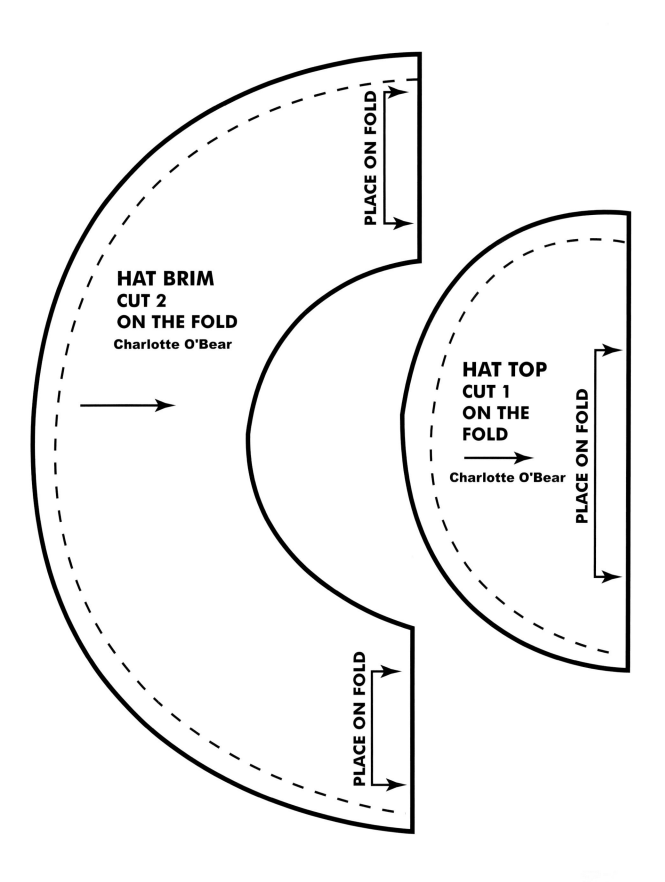

HAT BRIM
CUT 2
ON THE FOLD
Charlotte O'Bear

PLACE ON FOLD

PLACE ON FOLD

HAT TOP
CUT 1
ON THE
FOLD

Charlotte O'Bear

PLACE ON FOLD

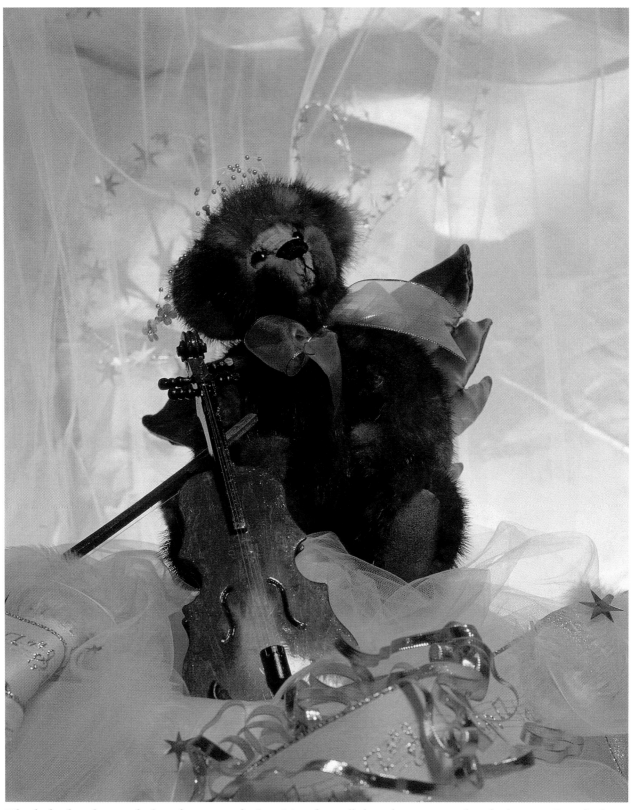

This little cherub is made from brown mink. It is 14 inches tall, has glass eyes, and quilted wings. I made the wings from the jacket's beautifully embroidered lining.

Project 6

Angel Bear

An angel can be defined as a benevolent being, messenger, or guardian, whose significance lies in its works. Over the years, I have received many orders for angels made from old fur coats. These cherub teddy bears serve as beautiful reminders of loved ones and bestow heartfelt love and kindness wherever they go.

Any teddy can be turned into an angel by simply adding wings. You will find instructions here for two types of wings: the first pair is made with feathers, and the second is quilted from the lining of a coat.

The angel bear design pictured here is 14 inches tall and made from brown mink. The quilted wings are made from the exquisitely embroidered lining of the coat and are trimmed with mocha-colored organza roses.

Close-up of the bear's face.

Angel bears make wonderful keepsakes and adorable gifts, especially at Christmas. Ring a little bell when your angel gets its wings and goes out into the world to fulfill its special purpose.

Follow the instructions in Chapters 3 through 6 to make your bear; there are also special instructions for this bear listed below.

Difficulty level: Easy to moderate

The back of the angel's wings show the fine embroidery which had been done on the lining.

ANGEL BEAR

You Will Need

1/4 yard of plush fabric or mohair or one fur stole or jacket
One set of eyes
One nose
Five sets of joints
6-inch square of fabric of your choice for paws
Stuffing
Scissors

Special Instructions

🐾 After stuffing, leave a 1/8-inch opening in the bottom of your teddy's back seam if you are going to use feather wings to insert the wire attachment.

FEATHER WINGS

You Will Need

Bristol board
24-gauge craft wire
Feathers
Scissors
Heavy-duty thread or monofilament

❶ Use the pattern to cut two pieces of bristol board. These will form the base of the wings.

Cut out the cardboard base.

❷ Fold a 10-inch section of wire in half. Wrap it around the center of one of the cardboard base pieces. Twist the two ends together at the bottom. Glue the two base pieces together and allow them to dry.

Wrap wire around the center of the pieces.

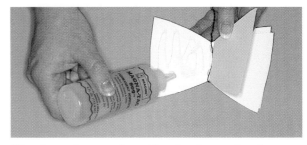

Glue the sections together with tacky glue or a hot glue gun.

❸ Glue five or six long feathers to both the right and left side of one side of the base. Follow this with a second row of shorter feathers. Allow the glue to dry.

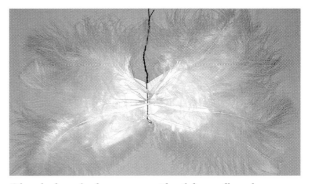

Glue the long feathers on one side of the cardboard.

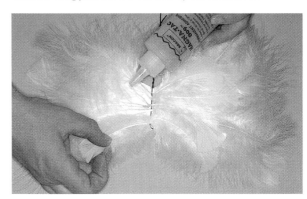

Glue a row of short feathers directly above the long ones.

④ On the other side of the base, arrange and glue on silk or parchment flowers, pearls, and ribbon trim. Allow the glue to dry before handling the wings.

Embellish the wings with flowers.

⑤ Bend the twisted wire end up against the feather side of the base. Place some tacky glue on this section of wire and insert it into the small hole you left while sewing the back seam. Using clear heavy-duty thread or monofilament, sew the wings onto the back using a large horizontal stitch around the center of the cardboard base. Adjust each stitch so the thread does not catch on the flowers.

Bend the wire back to allow the wings to be inserted into the bear's back seam. The wings should sit firmly against the bear. An additional dab of glue behind the wings will help hold them in place.

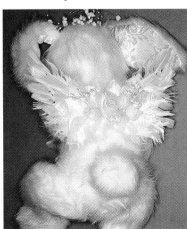

This particular angel bunny has a porcelain face. The fur is a shiny, synthetic plush, and the wings are trimmed with white organza rosettes.

Many types of ready-made wings are available at your local craft store.

Purchased wings can add variety to your work. Use your imagination to create your own heavenly teddy!

QUILTED WINGS

You Will Need

1/4 yard of fabric for quilted wings
Flowers, ribbon, and pearls
1/8 yard of quilt batting
Monofilament

① Use the pattern to cut two wings from fabric. Cut a rectangular section of quilt batting, large enough to cover the wings.

② Place the fabric wings, right sides together, on top of the batting and pin or baste all three layers together. You will have a layer of batting, followed by the two layers of fabric, with right sides together, on top. Sew around the entire outside edge of the wings through all layers. Trim all of the seam allowances to 1/8 inch, clip the curves, and trim the corners.

Use polyester batting for puffing up these quilted wings.

Sew and trim the edges.

❸ Cut a 2-inch long vertical slit through the center of the top layer of fabric. Turn the wings right side out through this slit. Press the seams. Sew a line of stitches on the quilting lines from the edge of the wing to the center as shown on the pattern markings. Fold the wings in half and stitch vertically down the center, 1/4 inch from the fold.

Cut a slit vertically up the center to allow the wings to be turned right side out.

❹ Using a whip stitch, sew the wings to the bear's center back. Use eight to ten stitches on each side. Decorate the center of the wings by sewing or gluing silk and organza flowers and ribbon along the fold.

Quilt the wings by sewing a row of stitching along the pattern's markings.

Sew a center seam.

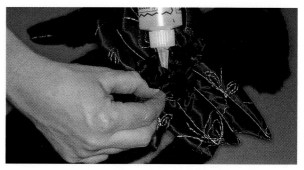

Decorate the wings with the desired blooms, buttons, ribbons, or other chosen accessories.

❺ Use a spray of pearls on clear monofilament for a halo. Bend the filament into several loops and secure these to the top of the bear's head with a stitch at each ear.

Attach the wings to the bear with a whip stitch.

~~~~~ *Tip* ~~~~~

When sewing or arranging the wings' placement, center them on the bear's back. If you place them too low on the angel's back, it will have problems sitting.

*O*no! It's sure is hard to fly! Wings need to be positioned in the center of your teddy's back to make sure it can fly!

This mink angel bear was made using the Classic Ted (short muzzle; see page 65) pattern. Here, I made the quilted wings from the coat's lining; the paws are also made from the lining.

I made this angel bear, Cygnus, from imported synthetic fur. I used the 14-inch Classic Ted pattern (long muzzle; see page 65), but this time I used ivory satin for the quilted wings.

For another idea, see the country angel on page 51. The wings are loops of raffia, gathered in the center and sewn to the bear's back.

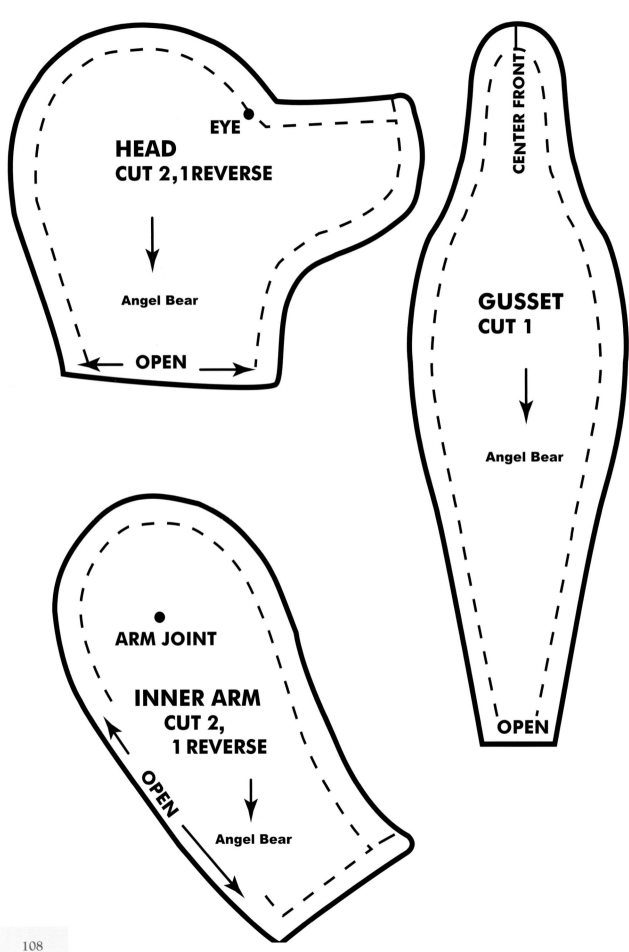

HEAD
CUT 2, 1 REVERSE

EYE

Angel Bear

OPEN

GUSSET
CUT 1

CENTER FRONT

Angel Bear

OPEN

INNER ARM
CUT 2,
1 REVERSE

ARM JOINT

OPEN

Angel Bear

108

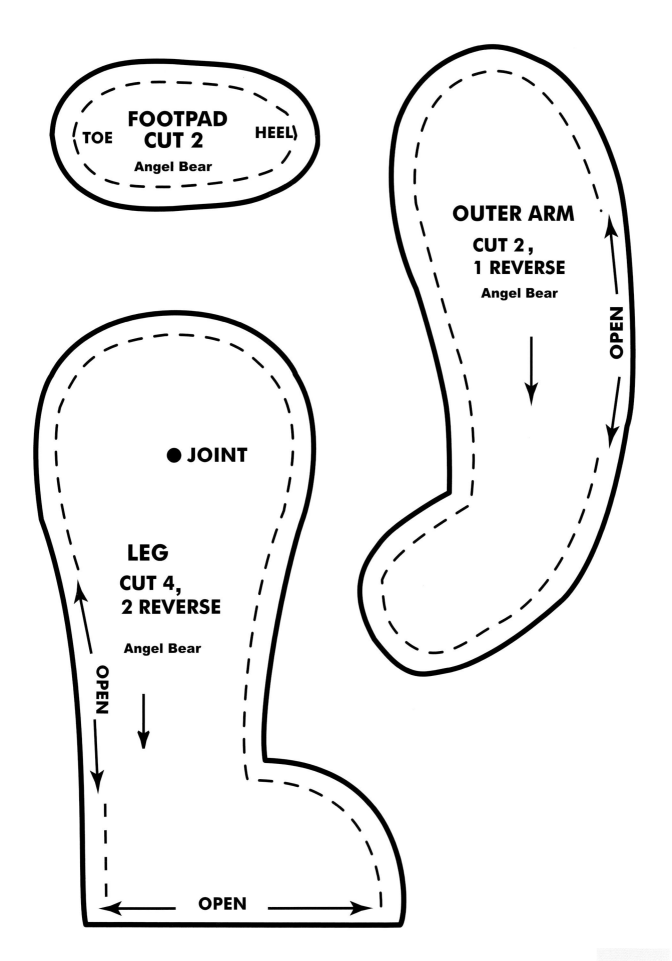

FOOTPAD
CUT 2

TOE   HEEL

Angel Bear

OUTER ARM

CUT 2,
1 REVERSE

Angel Bear

OPEN

● JOINT

LEG

CUT 4,
2 REVERSE

Angel Bear

OPEN

OPEN

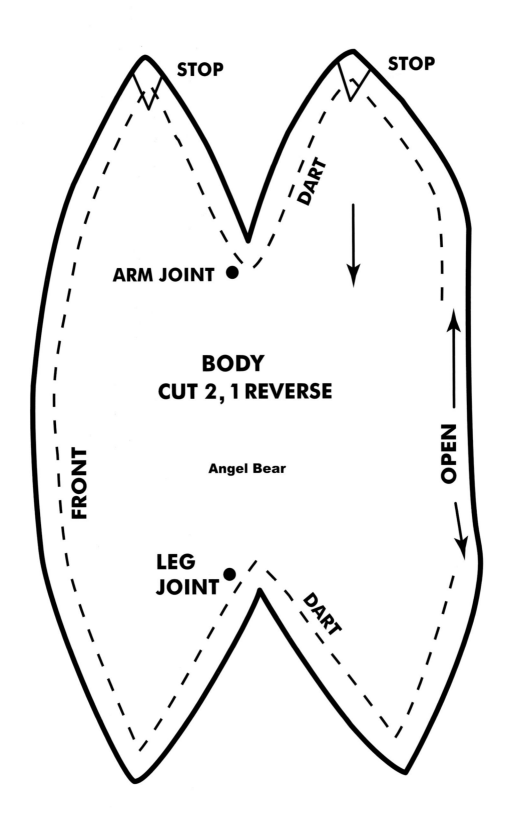

STOP

STOP

DART

ARM JOINT ●

BODY
CUT 2, 1 REVERSE

Angel Bear

FRONT

OPEN

LEG
JOINT ●

DART

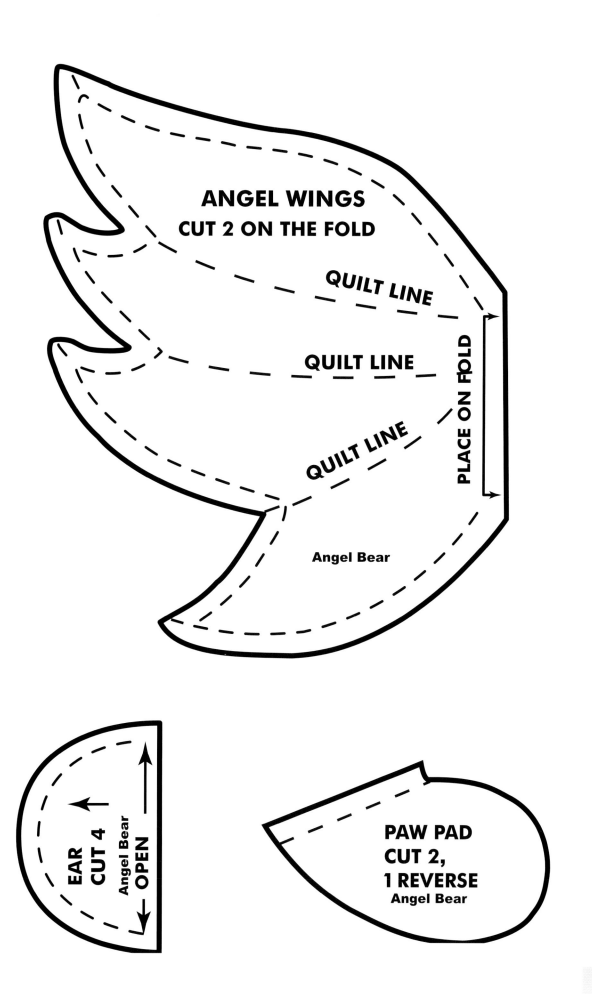

ANGEL WINGS
CUT 2 ON THE FOLD

QUILT LINE

QUILT LINE

QUILT LINE

PLACE ON FOLD

Angel Bear

EAR
CUT 4
Angel Bear
OPEN

PAW PAD
CUT 2,
1 REVERSE
Angel Bear

Truffles is a 15-inch bunny with flexible, wired ears. I used dark brown muskrat to make it. The muzzle is made from a contrasting white mink, and the ears and paws are satin.

This Bear's a Hare! "Truffles"

*I*f you have completed one or more of the projects in this book, congratulations! Now you may want to tackle a more advanced project. Truffles is well worth the little bit of extra effort it takes! This beautiful bunny uses all of the techniques taught in Chapters 3 through 6, as well as few new ones. Follow the instructions in Chapter 3 for laying out and cutting Truffles and the Special Instructions on the following page for completing the bunny. Follow the instructions in Chapter 4 for sewing the arms, legs, and body.

Truffles stands 15 inches tall, is fully jointed like the others, and is pictured here in muskrat with a mink contrasting muzzle. Its 6-inch ears are wired so they can be bent into many whimsical positions. I've used a pink pearl cotton to accent the nose. The ears, paws, and tail are lined with ivory satin, but you may also use the lining of your coat.

I especially enjoy my bear making time on long winter nights. These evenings are perfectly suited for tea and Truffles. So, sit down in your coziest spot with a cup of hot chocolate and bear making tools, and watch as your own hare-loom comes to life!

Difficulty level: Intermediate to advanced

THIS BEAR'S A HARE!
"TRUFFLES"

inches protrude from the ear. Repeat for the second ear. You will attach the ears in Step 4 of the next section.

Attach the wire to the seam allowance. Twist and trim the protruding wires.

You Will Need

1/3 yard of plush fabric or mohair or one fur stole or jacket

8-inch square of contrasting color fur for the muzzle

1/4 yard of lining or fabric for ears, paws, and tail

2 yards of 24-gauge craft wire

One set of eyes

One nose or pearl cotton

Five sets of joints

Stuffing

Ribbon and silk flowers for trim

Safety glasses

Special Instructions

❧ If you will be using the lining of your coat for the ears, paws, and tail, wash and press it before tracing and cutting out the pattern pieces.

❧ Finish your beautiful bunny with a wire-edge ribbon around its neck. Twist in the stem of a silk rose for a winsome appearance.

❧ The muzzle gusset and muzzle can be cut from contrasting fur.

SEWING THE EARS

❶ With right sides together, sew the lining to the fur portion of the ear. Leave the bottom straight edge open. Using a whip stitch or large machine zigzag stitch, attach craft wire to the ear's seam allowance. Go slowly if you are using the sewing machine so you do not break your needle by striking the wire. It is a good idea to wear safety glasses during this step, in case a needle breaks. Leave 6 inches of wire on each end protruding down from the ear. Repeat for the second ear.

Sew the ears.

❷ Carefully turn the ear right side out. Twist the two sections of wire together tightly. Smooth the wire around the ear with your fingers. Cut the ends of wire so that about 4

SEWING THE HEAD

❶ Sew the darts on either side of the bunny's muzzle using a 1/4-inch seam allowance. With right sides together, sew the two muzzle sections, from the tip of the nose as marked on the pattern to the bottom edge. Tack the center nose portion of the muzzle/gusset into the top of this seam. Hand sew the sides of the muzzle/gusset to the corresponding sides of the gusset using a backstitch.

Sew the darts in the muzzle.

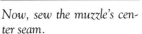

Now, sew the muzzle's center seam.

Attach the muzzle gusset to the muzzle.

❷ With the right sides together, sew the two head sections together from the lower muzzle opening to the base of the neck. Pin the gusset to the head sections, with right sides together. Be sure the muzzle end of the gusset matches the raw edges of the head at the top muzzle opening. Sew the gusset in place, leaving openings for the ears as marked on the pattern.

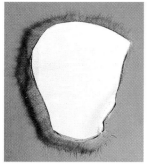

Sew the center head seam.

Attach the gusset to the head sections.

❸ With the right sides together, pin the muzzle to the head. Match up the neck seam and the center top markings. Sew the muzzle in place using a backstitch and heavy-duty thread.

Pin the muzzle to the head.

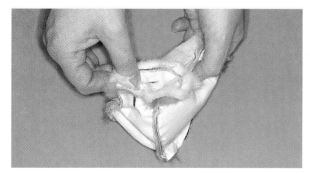

Sew the muzzle to the head.

❹ Place the ears into the openings from the inside (right side) of the head. Sew the opening shut using doubled heavy-duty thread and a backstitch. The wires should protrude to the outside (wrong side) of the head. Be sure when attaching the ears that the satin side of the ears will fall outward when the bunny's head is right side out. Turn the head right side out and check the positioning before sewing.

The ears' lining should always face outward.

❺ Twist the two protruding wire clusters together. Leave about 1/2 inch near the gusset on either wire untwisted so the head does not pucker together when you turn it right side out. Wrap a wad of polyester fiberfill around the wire and secure it with a thread tied in various spots along its length.

❻ Turn the head right side out. Stuff the remainder of the head to the desired firmness. Be sure to evenly distribute the stuffing around the inner wire so the head feels soft and the wire does not poke out.

❼ Finish the rest of the head by following the instructions in Chapter 5. When embroidering the nose, place it over the point where the gusset meets the center muzzle seam (see page 41 for information on embroidering noses).

MAKING THE TAIL

❶ With right sides together, sew the satin lining to the fur section of the tail. Turn the tail right side out. Close the lower edge using a whip stitch.

❷ Sew the tail to the body using a whip stitch through all layers of the fabric. Sew along the top of the tail first. Follow this by a row of stitches along the bottom of the tail. The tail is attached on an angle on either side of the center back seam. The pattern markings will help you with the tail placement.

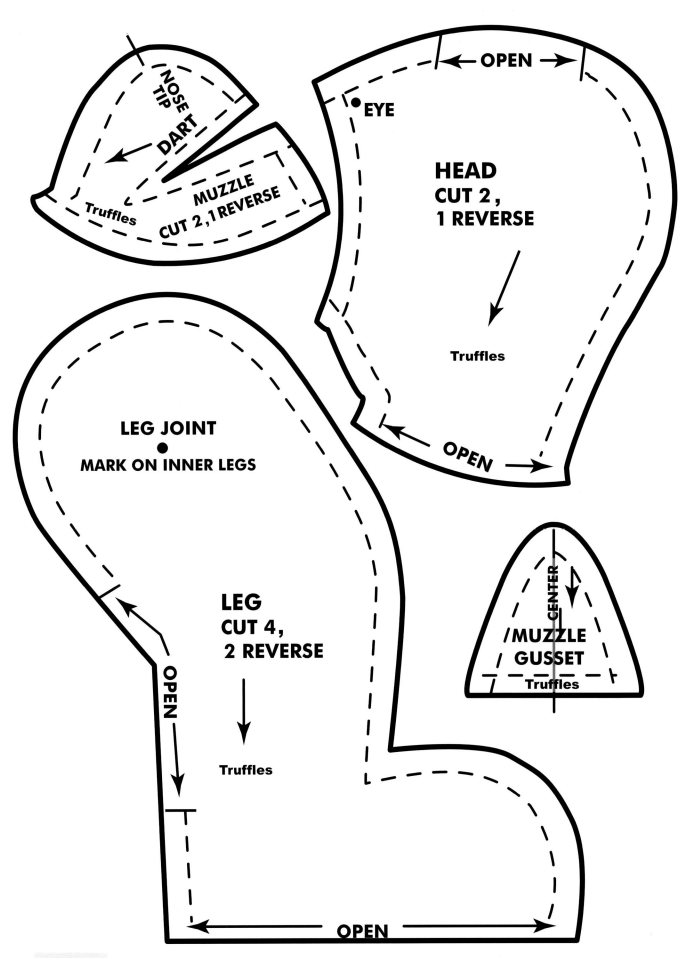

NOSE TIP

DART

Truffles

MUZZLE
CUT 2, 1 REVERSE

OPEN

EYE

HEAD
CUT 2,
1 REVERSE

Truffles

OPEN

LEG JOINT
MARK ON INNER LEGS

LEG
CUT 4,
2 REVERSE

Truffles

OPEN

OPEN

CENTER

MUZZLE
GUSSET
Truffles

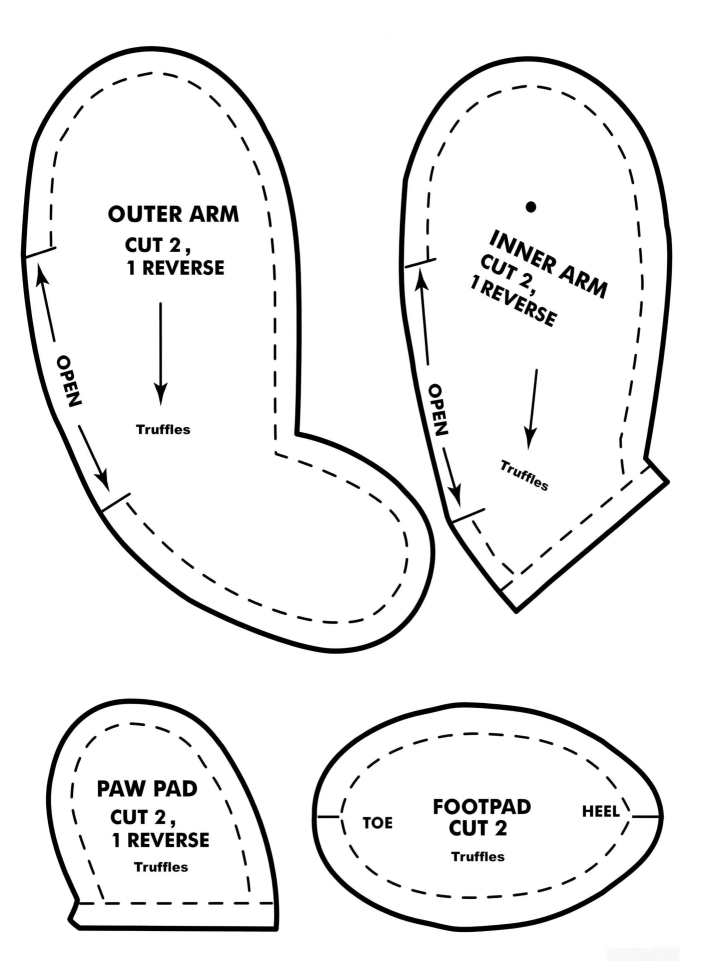

OUTER ARM
CUT 2 ,
1 REVERSE

OPEN

Truffles

INNER ARM
CUT 2,
1 REVERSE

OPEN

Truffles

PAW PAD
CUT 2,
1 REVERSE

Truffles

FOOTPAD
CUT 2

TOE

HEEL

Truffles

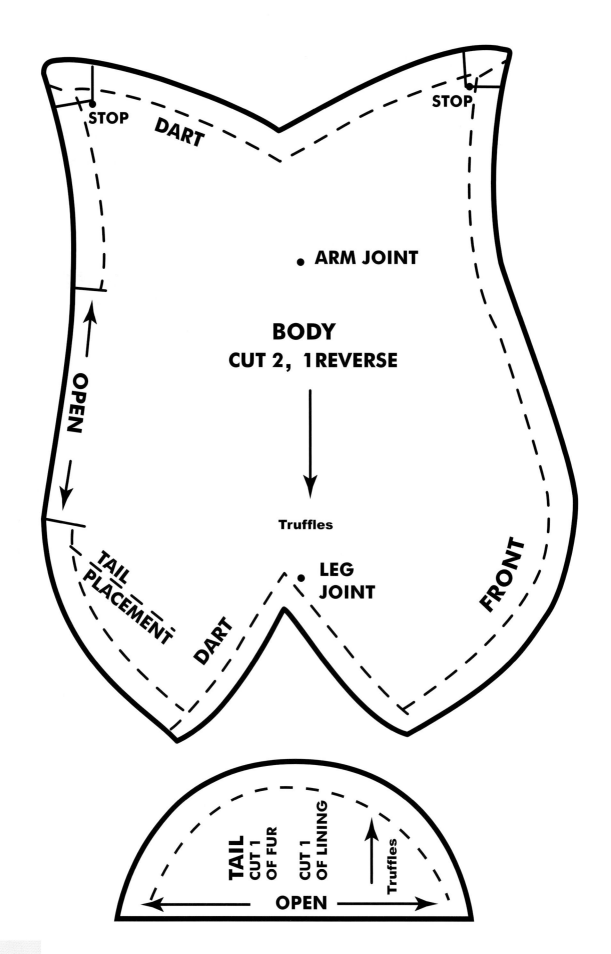

STOP

STOP

DART

ARM JOINT

BODY
CUT 2, 1 REVERSE

OPEN

Truffles

TAIL
PLACEMENT

DART

LEG
JOINT

FRONT

TAIL
CUT 1
OF FUR

CUT 1
OF LINING

Truffles

OPEN

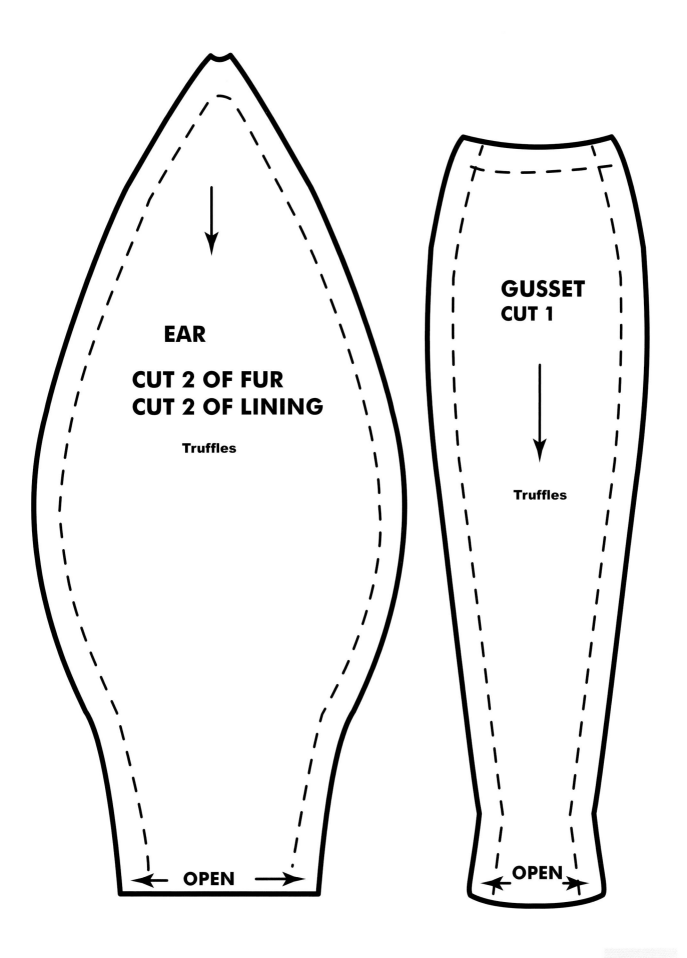

EAR

CUT 2 OF FUR
CUT 2 OF LINING

Truffles

OPEN

GUSSET
CUT 1

Truffles

OPEN

Can't figure out what to do with your scraps? Make an ornament! This is the Santa Bear Christmas Ornament.

Ladies and gentlemen make fancy pins. I used German synthetic plush scraps to make them.

Project 8

Inventive Scrap Creations

I often receive calls from people who own fur hats and collars and would like teddy bears made from them. Although it is possible to make small bears from collars, the general rule for real fur is that the smaller the teddy bear, the more difficult it is to make.

Another quandary I face on a regular basis is what to do with my mohair scraps. At the current price, it does not take long before I'm ready to throw a few hundred dollars worth of waste into the garbage. Rather than make small bears from these tiny pieces of fabric, why not make just a teddy bear head in a more reasonable size?

This chapter is designed for every level of experience and will allow you to really use your ingenuity as you create pins and ornaments to suit your needs. The sky is the limit when it comes to the characters you can create! Have fun!

Difficulty level: Easy

Inventive Scrap Creations

Pin

The handsome gentleman is wearing a purchased top hat. His collar and bow tie are made from scraps of felt and satin ribbon. The lovely lady's hat is made from scraps of netting, fun foam, and feathers. These were all leftovers from Auntie Bear-nadette, on page 85. I glued a string of faux pearls to her neck for a touch of elegance.

The nurse's hat is made from scraps of felt and black ribbon. The spectacles are made of 24-gauge craft wire bent around a pencil to give the lenses a round shape.

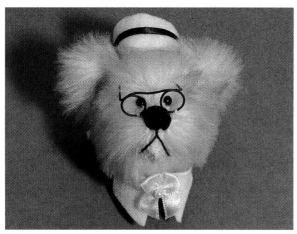

This nurse pin was made from pink-tipped mohair. I made her glasses from 24-gauge craft wire bent around a pencil and her hat from felt.

You Will Need

Scraps of fur, plush fabric, or mohair
Muslin to line real fur
One pair of eyes
One nose or pearl cotton
Pearl cotton for the mouth
Flowers and ribbon for trim
Pin back

❶ Transfer the pattern to the back of your scrap fur, plush or mohair. If using real fur, be sure to line each piece with muslin as described in Chapter 3.

❷ With right sides together, sew the two head sections together from the tip on the nose to the bottom of the opening marked at the back of the head. Tack the center of the nose portion of the gusset to this seam at the nose. Pin each side of the gusset to the corresponding side of the head. Sew this in place with heavy-duty thread and a back-stitch.

Sew the head seam.   *Attach the gusset; leave an opening in the back.*

❸ If you choose to use safety eyes or a safety nose, insert them now, following the instructions in Chapter 5.

❹ Turn the head right side out and stuff it to the desired firmness. Sew a running stitch around the opening and pull it tight to close it. Sew any small spaces shut with a whip stitch. Knot off the thread and bury the end of the thread in the head.

❺ To make the ears, fold the ear piece in half with right sides together and sew all around the curved edge. Cut a small, horizontal slit directly on the fold. Turn the ear right side out through this slit. Sew the ears to the head using a whip stitch. The nap of the fur should run up at the front of the ear and down along the back of the ear.

Fold and sew the ear.   *Cut a slit in the fold; turn the ear through this opening.*

6 Using heavy-duty thread, sew the pin back to the back of the head. Finish the face using the instructions in Chapter 5 for attaching glass eyes and the ears, and embroidering a nose.

Attach the pin back with heavy-duty thread.

SANTA ORNAMENT

For this unique ornament, use the instructions in Chapter 3 for the pattern layout. If you are using scraps of fur, pay special attention to the direction of the nap. Construct the teddy bear head using the instructions in Chapters 4 and 5. Close the bottom of the head by sewing a running stitch around the open edge with heavy-duty thread. Pull the thread to close the neck opening and secure the thread with a knot.

You Will Need

Scraps of fur, plush fabric, or mohair
Muslin for lining real fur
One pair of eyes
One nose or pearl cotton
Pearl cotton for the mouth
10-inch square of red velveteen, a bell, and a sprig of artificial holly

1 Cut a 7-inch diameter circle from the velveteen. Cut this circle in half. To make the cape, use pinking shears or a serger to finish the edges of one of the half circles. Sew a narrow strip of fur to its curved edge.

2 Sew a running stitch along the straight edge and gather it so it measures 1-1/2 inches long. Sew this gathered edge to the neck of the teddy bear, so the open edge is at the center front. Glue a sprig of holly to the neck edge of the cape.

3 For the hat, cut the remaining half circle in half again so that you have two quarter circles. With right sides together, sew the straight edges together so your quarter circle becomes a cone. Glue or sew a narrow strip of fur around the base of the cone. Sew a bell to the top of the cone.

4 Sew or glue the hat onto the Santa. Stitch a length of ribbon to the top of Santa's head to hang on your Christmas tree.

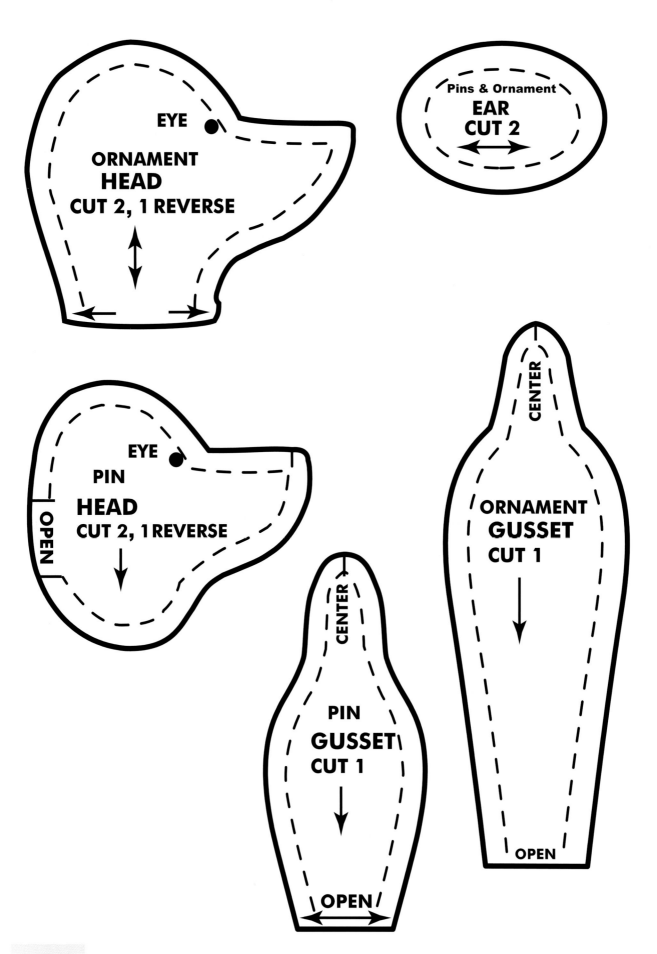

EYE

**ORNAMENT HEAD
CUT 2, 1 REVERSE**

Pins & Ornament
**EAR
CUT 2**

EYE

PIN

OPEN

**HEAD
CUT 2, 1 REVERSE**

CENTER

**ORNAMENT
GUSSET
CUT 1**

CENTER

**PIN
GUSSET
CUT 1**

OPEN

OPEN

Chapter 8

Questions and Answers

Whenever I am lecturing or presenting my teddy bears at shows, I am approached by people who have fur coats at home and have questions about turning them into a teddy bear. My workshop students also have many questions. In this chapter, I have listed many of the most commonly asked questions and provided the answers for you. The questions deal with the age of coats, cleaning them, storing bears, grooming a finished teddy, and a host of other tips not already mentioned in this book.

I don't have a fur coat. Where can I get one?

Used fur coats are not hard to find. I am constantly on the lookout for them in thrift shops, second-hand ladies' wear stores, and at auctions, estate sales, and yard sales. Ask your friends! You may be surprised to find what they have in their attics. Check the classified section of your local newspaper between August and May; often people will try to sell their coats then. In the past I have run newspaper ads, saying that I was looking for old fur coats. One ad resulted in more than one hundred phone calls in a week! Also, your local furrier may be an excellent source of information in terms of who's selling. Finally, if you have access to the Internet, check auction web sites. You'll find a bounty of fur coats to bid on!

How much should I pay for a coat?

Fur coats, like many cars, depreciate with age; however, because of the enormous sentimental value some people attach to coats, the price tags may be quite high, even on very old coats. Generally, I will not pay more than $100 for a coat that is more than ten years old. I do make exceptions for full-length coats in very good condition or made from unusual furs. Your top dollar may vary, depending on the condition of the coat and the number of bears that can be made from it.

How many bears can be made from a coat?

This depends on several factors. The size of the coat, the size of the bear, and the condition of the coat all play a role in determining the number of teddies you can make. On one occasion, I made seven 14-inch teddy bears from one size 16 full-length coat. Most stoles will make a 15- to 17-inch teddy or two 10-inch tall bears.

Is there any type of fur that is very easy to work with?

Yes. If you are just beginning to make real fur bears, I suggest using seal, rabbit, mink, or muskrat. See the chart on page 22 to help you choose the fur that is best for your ability level or use plush fabric or mohair.

Can I make a bear from a fur that is very dry and tears easily?

Yes! Follow the instructions in Chapter 3 for pattern layout, and don't forget to wipe a thin layer of glycerin on the pelts to help soften them (see page 23). Lining dry pelts is crucial! Now, if you still have a tear, glue the pelt down against the lining inside the bear, and voilà! No one will ever know. Remember that old coats will make fragile teddies. I do not recommend that these bears be played with or hugged too tightly!

I've heard that fur coats can be infested with bugs. If this is so, can I still use the coat?

Because it is made of animal fur, an old fur coat can be an attractive nesting site for pests, the most common of which are mites. To destroy all pests, simply wrap the coat tightly in a plastic bag with a mothball and leave it for one to two weeks. You could also place the bag in the freezer without a mothball. Shake the coat out afterward and air it out outdoors. After you have cut out your pattern pieces, be sure to run your vacuum over all of the edges, the backs of the pelts, and the fur itself. Wear a dust mask to protect yourself from inhaling dust and other particles.

Should I have my coat professionally cleaned before I begin?

This is not usually necessary; however, if you have purchased the coat from a thrift shop or yard sale, it may be desirable. Cleaning is quite reasonably priced and may make you more comfortable when you hug your teddy.

My coat smells funny. How can I get rid of the odor?

I have found that for coats that smell of cigarette smoke, a professional cleaning is the only answer. The smell of mold or mildew is difficult to remove. Try putting the coat in a plastic bag for a week with one or two baking soda tablets. Alternatively, there are now several spray-on products on the market that will remove odors. Read the label and test the product on a small portion of the fur before spraying the entire coat. A professional cleaning may be your best solution, though. You can also place the coat in a dryer on the fluff cycle with a scented softening sheet. Do not use a heat setting!

I don't know what kind of fur my coat is made of. How can I find out?

Take your coat to a furrier, who will be able to identify it for you, or try to call the furrier with a description of your coat. If there is no furrier in your area, ask your friends; someone may know! Compare your coat to others you may see pictured on auction sites on the Internet.

Can I mix different furs within a teddy bear?

This depends on the look you are after. Furs can be mixed, but the resulting teddy bear may look mismatched. If you are going to mix and match, I suggest trading colors within the same fur species. For example, use light and dark shades of mink, or black and white fur, as shown on page 76. For the true artist, mixing various types of fur can be a wonderful experience in creative expression.

I don't have enough fur for a teddy bear in my collar. Can I mix it with a synthetic fur?

Yes, by all means add synthetics or mohair to your real fur project. Remember that genuine fur needs to be lined, but the others do not. Try to keep the furs similar in texture: use short furs with short synthetics and long with long. Try mixing the two as a panda bear (see page 79).

My mohair teddy's hair is out of control! How can I get the fur to go where I want it?

Moisten a washcloth with cool water. Rub this over the mohair so it, but not the stuffing, becomes damp. Brush the fur in the direction you want it to go. Tape it into place with Scotch or masking tape. When the fur dries, remove the tape and give your teddy another grooming. The fur will now be "trained" to go in the direction you chose.

I can't seem to get the needle through the fur sections when I'm hand sewing. Can you recommend anything to make it easier?

Keep a small pair of needle nose pliers on hand. Grip the needle with the pliers to push it through the layers of fur. Then, grip the needle on the other side and pull it through. This method takes a little extra time, but saves a great deal of wear and tear on your fingers, especially if you are working with very thick pelts.

Is there an easy way to sew on my teddy's ears?

It is important to make sure your bear's ears are securely fastened because many people who admire it will pick it up by the ears. Many of my students prefer using a curved needle because they tell me it pops right back up where they want it. You can also use a ladder stitch to secure the back of the ear to the head. The bottom opening of the ear must be sewn shut first. The natural curve of the head will cause the ear to pop right up into the proper position.

Are there any special care requirements for my finished bear?

Yes. Keep it out of direct sunlight and away from extremes in heat and humidity. All of the teddy bears I know hate dirt and dust. Cover the crevice tool of your vacuum cleaner with a nylon stocking and vacuum your creation once a month. This should be all the cleaning your bear will need.

Natural fur bears will act as a sponge for strong cooking odors and smoke. Cover it with a plastic or glass container if it is an heirloom. If you are covering it temporarily, use a paper bag. Never store it in a plastic bag; it will suffocate and you may damage the fur.

How can I personalize my bear?

There are many different ways to do this. I have had students embroider "Love ____" (fill in name) on a paw pad. Sometimes, monograms removed from the fur coat can be attached to a paw pad or a bow. I sew a tag with my trade name "Kran-Beary's" sewn across the right paw of all of my bears.

Where can I see more bears and learn more about bear making?

Check your local bookstore for magazines; there are several from around the world that deal specifically with teddy bears. In them, you will find a wealth of information about suppliers, artists, and upcoming shows and conventions. You may find you have an expert teddy bear artist living very near you who would love to help you explore this exciting hobby further. If you have access to the Internet, try searching "real fur teddy bears" or even just "teddy bears." You will find thousands of web sites related to the subject. Many teddy bear supply shops offer workshops by prominent artists. If you have the opportunity to take a workshop, by all means, do it! Every artist has his or her own set of tips and secrets to pass onto you.

Is there more than one method I can use to make a teddy bear?

Absolutely. Every artist will have a slightly different technique. In this book, I have shown you what works well for me, and what my customers and students find attractive and workable. But, you might devise your own special secrets to bear making!

Supplies and Sources

The following is a listing of some outstanding teddy bear supply outlets, where you can purchase teddy bear making supplies and fur in North America. Contact them for more information or to request a catalog. Also check your local craft supply store for supplies.

Dear Bears Market Place
4747 Quebec Street
Vancouver, British Columbia, Canada V5V 3M2
Phone: (604) 872-2508 or 888-823-2327
Fax: (604) 872-2504
Web site: www.dear-bears.com
E-mail: dearbear@istar.ca
Carries synthetic plush, mohair, and genuine reclaimed fur, teddy bear making supplies for all sizes of bears, and a line of French velour fabrics specifically for teddy bear making.

Disco Joints and Teddies
2 Ridgewood Place
St. Clements, Ontario, Canada N0B 2M0
Phone: (519) 699-5762
Fax: (519) 699-4525
Web site: www.discojoints.on.ca
E-mail: disco@discojoints.on.ca
Carries mohair, synthetic plush, and a wide variety of teddy bear making supplies.

Edinburgh Imports
P.O. Box 340
Newbury Park, California 91319-0340
Showroom at:
1121 Lawrence Drive
Newbury Park, California 91320
Phone: (805) 376-1700
Fax: (805) 376-1711
Web site: www.edinburgh.com
E-mail: rblock@edinburgh.com
Carries more than 1,000 mohair and fabric varieties and all teddy bear making supplies. Has a 36-page catalog.

Intercal Trading Group
1760 Monrovia Suite A-17
Costa Mesa, California 92627
Phone: (949) 645-9396
Fax: (949) 645-5471
Web site: www.intercaltg.com
Carries hundreds of mohair and fabric varieties and teddy bear making supplies.

Out of Hand Ltd.
#1-3919 Richmond Road S.W.
Calgary, Alberta, Canada T3E 4P2
Phone: (403) 217-4871 or 888-263-3353
Fax: (403) 249-1778
Web site: www.out-of-hand.com
E-mail: Dei@nucleus.com
Carries bear making supplies for all sizes and styles of bears.

Spare Bear Parts
Box 56P
Interlochen, Michigan 49643
Phone: (231) 276-7915
Fax: (231) 276-7921
Web site: www.SpareBear.com
E-mail: sales@SpareBear.com
Carries joints, glass eyes, music boxes, growlers, and bear making supplies. The company is a direct importer of mohair and carries synthetic plush fabrics selected specifically for making teddy bears.

2-Bears Teddy Bears
1904-20 Avenue N.W.
Calgary, Alberta, Canada Y2M 1H5
Phone: (403) 282-4770 or 888-288-4770
Fax: (403) 282-9234
Web site: www.2bearsltd.com
E-mail: info@2bearsltd.com
Carries a large selection of imported mohair and synthetic plush, all teddy bear making supplies, and a large gallery of manufactured teddy bears for sale.

Glossary

Some of the terms listed in here were already covered in Chapter 2; refer to page 15 for definitions.

Acrylic plush: A fur-like fabric woven from acrylic fibers which are produced synthetically and give additional strength and durability to the coat.

Awl: A tool with a very sharp, pointed end used to poke holes through fabric in a teddy bear.

Black lining: See page 15.

Cotter pin: A two-pronged metal pin used to attach disk joints in a teddy bear's limbs.

Excelsior (Wood wool): A name used for wood shavings. These shavings were commonly used to stuff teddy bears early in the twentieth century.

Fiberboard: Compressed wood pulp, often used to manufacture the disks used in teddy bear joints.

Growler: A cylindrical voice box which is inserted into the teddy and produces a growling-type noise when the bear is tipped.

Guard hairs: See page 15.

Interfacing: A fabric used to stabilize another fabric. Some types have a fusible side which can be ironed onto the fabric. It is available in fabric stores.

Kapok: A lightweight stuffing made from the fibers of a tropical tree's seed pods.

Leather (Animal hide): See page 15.

Mites: Microscopic parasites that feed on dust.

Mohair: The wool of the angora goat. Woven into a plush fur-type fabric, it is ideal for making teddy bears.

Pearl cotton: A woven cotton sold on spools and in skeins. The fibers are not easily separated, making it the perfect choice for embroidered teddy bear noses.

Pelt seams: See page 15.

Pelted coat: See page 15.

Pelts (Skins): See page 15.

Pile (Plush): Fibers that stand out from the woven backing, resembling fur.

Safety parts: Eyes, noses, and joints that fasten with a locking washer, making removal difficult.

Shoe buttons: Molded black buttons with a hook on the back. They were used extensively for fastening shoes and boots early in the twentieth century and make wonderful teddy bear eyes.

Soft sculpture: A technique used in producing stuffed animals and dolls. Several stitches, hidden from the exterior view, result in a change in the shape of the finished product.

Synthetic: A manmade substance.

Ultrasuede: Trade name for a synthetic faux suede. It is ideal for making bear paws.

Undercoat (Under fur): See page 15.

Index